MAGNA CARTA
in Essex

Andrew Summers
John Debenham

Published by Summersbook (UK) Ltd
Essex Hundred Publications
Rutland House
90 – 92 Baxter Avenue
Southend-on-Sea
Essex SS2 6HZ
www.essex100.com

Magna Carta in Essex
First published June 2015
Written by Andrew Summers and John Debenham
© Copyright Andrew Summers and John Debenham
June 2015
All rights reserved.

British library cataloguing in Publication Data:
A catalogue record for this book is available from
The British Library.

ISBN 9780993108303

Typeset by Hutchins Creative Limited
Printed by 4edge Publishing
7a Eldon Way
Eldon Way Industrial Estate
Hockley Essex SS5 4AD

England and France in approximately 1200

PEMBROKE

HEREFORD ● ● WORCESTER

MONMOUTH ●

ENGLAND

BURY ST EDMONDS

COLCHESTER

ST ALBANS **ESSEX**

LONDON

SALISBURY CANTERBURY

EXETER CHICHESTER HASTINGS DOVER

FLANDERS

BOUVINES

CHERBOURG

CHANNEL ISLANDS

ROUEN

LAON

BAYEUX ● CAEN

R. SEINE PARIS

NORMANDY

BRITTANY

CHARTRES

BLOIS

R. LOIRE TOURS

ANJOU

CHINON

● POITIERS

POITOU

LA ROCHELLE

LIMOGES

ANGOULÊME

AQUITAINE

R. DORDOGNE

BORDEAUX

The English King had extensive lands in Normandy,
Anjou, Poitou and Aquitaine.
By 1204 Normandy had been lost.

To no one will we sell,
to no one deny
or delay right or justice.

Contents

Page no

7	List of Illustrations and Maps
11	Introduction
14	Acknowledgements
15	Glossary
18	Principal Characters
20	The Chroniclers
21	Excommunication
22	Kings and Barons
25	The English Countryside
26	The Great Forest of Essex
31	Tipping Point
33	The Road to Runnymede
35	June 15th 1215
37	War
39	The King's Mercenary
45	Historical Note. Mountfitchet Castle
48	The King Returns
52	Death of a King
55	The Battle for the Crown of England
60	The Barons
64	A Small World
65	Charter of the Forest
67	The Demise of Essex Forest
71	The Last Forest
72	Unusual (Essex) Connections
74	Full Text of Magna Carta
84	Full Text of the Forest Charter
88	Selected bibliography
90	Authors
91	Essex Hundred Publications

A reproduction of the Magna Carta text at Little Dunmow showing the Great Seal of King John.

List of Illustrations and Maps

(All maps and images are from the Essex100 collection
unless otherwise noted)

Front and back cover. *We are all Witness* as Robert Fitzwalter leader of the council of twenty five watches King John sealing the Magna Carta. Created in Bath stone by David Parfitt and installed at Egham Town Centre in June 1994.

3	Map. England and France around 1200
6	Facsimile of Magna Carta
8/9	Map of Essex 1215
10	Castle Hedingham Courtesy of Castle Hedingham Archives
24	Dürnstein Castle
30	Matilda (Maid Marion)
44	Map. Route of Savary de Mauléon's Chevauchées in Essex.
45	Inside Mountfitchet Castle
46/47	Runnymede Hall, Thundersley, Colchester Castle, Robert Fitzwalter, Robert de Vere, Gravestones Tilty, Stansted Mountfitchet sign
51	Map. King John in Essex 1216
63	Geoffrey de Mandeville of Pleshey Image courtesy of Palace of Westminster Collection, WOA S40
70	The Peoples Forest. Epping
71	Hatfield Broad Oak Church in 1800
73	The King John School, Runnymede Chase/ Runnymede Road
83	St Nicholas Chapel, Coggeshall
89	The Remains of Pleshey Castle

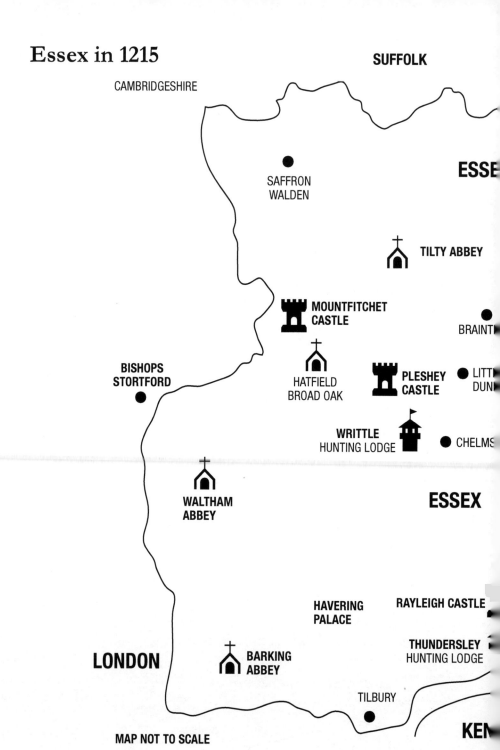

Essex in 1215

SUFFOLK

CAMBRIDGESHIRE

ESSE

SAFFRON
WALDEN

TILTY ABBEY

MOUNTFITCHET
CASTLE

BRAINT

BISHOPS
STORTFORD

HATFIELD
BROAD OAK

PLESHEY
CASTLE

LITTI
DUNI

WRITTLE
HUNTING LODGE

CHELMS

WALTHAM
ABBEY

ESSEX

HAVERING
PALACE

RAYLEIGH CASTLE

LONDON

BARKING
ABBEY

THUNDERSLEY
HUNTING LODGE

TILBURY

KEN

MAP NOT TO SCALE

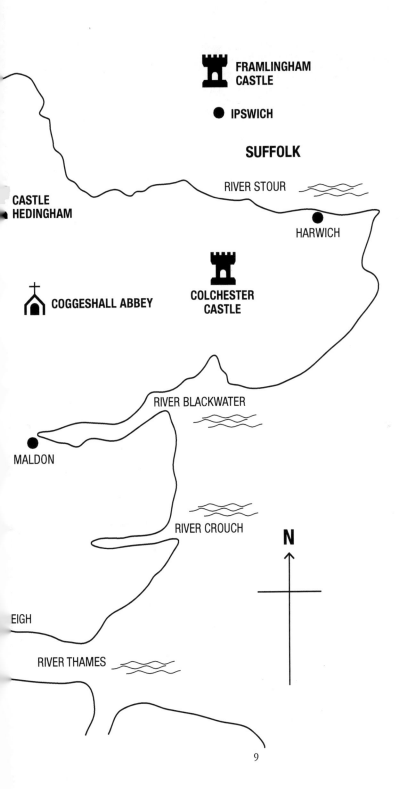

FRAMLINGHAM
CASTLE

● IPSWICH

SUFFOLK

RIVER STOUR

CASTLE
HEDINGHAM

HARWICH

COGGESHALL ABBEY

COLCHESTER
CASTLE

RIVER BLACKWATER

● MALDON

RIVER CROUCH

N

EIGH

RIVER THAMES

Castle Hedingham, the Essex home of Robert de Vere

Introduction

In writing this book it was never our intention to create an academic reference work. Rather, we examine the events and background leading up to the sealing of the Magna Carta by King John in the year 1215. We look particularly at the status of Essex at the time, the role of its powerful nobility and the consequential effects on the county of this historic event. Even today these consequences reverberate in our legal system and our most basic rights. In a few pages we have tried to summarise the above as concisely and as simply as possible.

Many readers may be familiar with two of Magna Carta's most famous clauses:-

39. No free man shall be seized or imprisoned, or stripped of his rights or possessions, or outlawed or exiled, or deprived of his standing in any way, nor will we proceed with force against him, or send others to do so, except by the lawful judgment of his equals or by the law of the land.

40. To no one will we sell, to no one deny or delay right or justice.

Yet these are only two of some 61 clauses set down in order of ranking. They have been quoted frequently at turning points during English history such as the trial and execution of King Charles I and the arrival of William and Mary, followed by Queen Anne, after the 'Glorious Revolution'. These two clauses are pillars of the US constitution. However the word 'free men' is open to misinterpretation. In 1776, in the United States, slaves were not 'free men' so the clause did not apply. This was also the case in feudal England where, in 1215 and for many years after, most people who worked on the land were in servitude to their baronial masters.

There are three other clauses in the Magna Carta that were perhaps of particular interest to the inhabitants of Essex;-

44. People who live outside the forest need not in future appear before the royal justices of the forest in answer to general summonses unless they are actually involved in proceedings or are sureties for someone who has been seized for a forest offence.

47. All forests that have been created in our reign shall at once be disafforested. River-banks that have been enclosed in our reign shall be treated similarly.

48. All evil customs relating to forests and warrens, foresters, warreners, sheriffs and their servants, or river-banks and their wardens, are at once to be investigated in every county by twelve sworn knights of the county, and within forty days of their enquiry the evil customs are to be abolished completely and irrevocably.

These three clauses were significant since, when the Magna Carta was sealed in 1215, practically the whole of Essex was designated 'forest'. The origin of the word forest comes from the Latin, forestis, meaning outside. Forest then did not simply mean an area of densely wooded oak and beech, picturesque glades and clearings such as, for example, Epping Forest is today. The medieval 'forest' was an area of unenclosed countryside. Forest land could be wooded, part agricultural with meadows or just plain heath or scrub land and could even include towns and villages. Perhaps more sinister, it was an area where 'Forest Laws' applied. These were laws separate and distinct from those of the central administration and outside the common law and where the monarch's word was arbitrary and final. All who lived and worked in the forest were subject to the 'Forest Laws', which were superior to all other courts of the land.

One of the conditions of the agreement with the king was that twenty five barons should be selected and be charged with ensuring that the king respected the charter. Their leader was Robert Fitzwalter, Lord of Dunmow. The group included four more Essex figures; Richard de Montfitchet, Sheriff of Essex, Geoffrey de Mandeville of Pleshey, William de Lanvallei, the Governor of Colchester Castle, and Robert de Vere of Castle Hedingham. Curiously, in 1215, Richard de Montfitchet owned the land at Runnymede where the Magna Carta was sealed and the words 'Magna Carta A-D-1215' appear on the village sign at Stansted Montfitchet.

Shortly after the Magna Carta was sealed King John reneged on it supported by the pope who not only annulled it but excommunicated the twenty-five barons. It may never have survived if it hadn't been for the unexpected death of King John, in Newark in October, 1216. John left England, in a state of anarchy and civil war, to be ruled by his nine year old son Henry III. To bring about a semblance of order William Marshall, who was appointed as regent to the boy king, hastily issued a modified version of the

Magna Carta. This appeased the warring barons and resulted, some would say, in miraculously restoring a degree of order and unity to the kingdom.

It is worth noting that whilst the Magna Carta was written down 800 years ago and underwrites much of our legal system, England (and its successor the United Kingdom) still has no written constitution or singular bill of rights.

As for Essex; the county's woodland forests are a fraction of their former size, due to constant attack from commercial interests since the early 1800s. These forests, and the numerous parklands that we enjoy, owe their survival to principals laid down in the Magna Carta and to the heroic efforts of a handful of determined individuals.

After 1066, when William Duke of Normandy took the English crown at the battle of Hastings, English and French royalty, baronial families and territories became evermore intertwined. Successive English monarchs reigned over large areas of modern day central and western France (see map page 3). There were numerous disputes and rival claims to both the English and French thrones which frequently led to wars. During the time frame of the Magna Carta, the French had become more assertive. At the same time King John battled constantly to retain his French lands. This situation continued for centuries until England lost its last French enclave, Calais, during the reign of Queen Mary in 1558. Despite this loss England still claimed the right to the French crown for another 250 years.

Ten years after the French Revolution overthrew the French monarchy in 1792, George III, the king of newly created Great Britain and Ireland, dropped his claim to the French throne and Britain fully recognised the French Republic in 1802.

History can be confusing! On a confusing note, to be helpful a glossary of some of the medieval terms that have largely fallen out of use is given on pages 15, 16 and 17.

Acknowledgements

In bringing this book to publication we have benefited greatly from the help of curators, archivists, editors, librarians and many others throughout the county. Without them the book would not have been possible and we are indebted to them.

Establishing the detail of some of the events we relate has been a complex process. Researching this material so far back in time has been a challenge. Much of the source material is in Latin or French and events surroundings the Magna Carta and its Essex connections have been disputed, argued over, reinterpreted and speculated on by chroniclers of the day and historians through the ages.

We have taken every care to check facts, however we are aware that we are fallible. For any errors found in our text we humbly apologise. Should any reader be able to provide additional information to enlighten us on any chapters in the book, their comments would be most welcome and we offer our thanks in advance.

We would like to give special mention to Jane Greatorex of Castle Hedingham for the background to the castle and enlightening us on the curious aspects of medieval sieges and *parleys*. Peter Sanders was very helpful with the events surrounding Mountfitchet's castle and local town signage. Professor Nigel Saul, the Head of the Department of History at Royal Holloway University of London, gave valuable information in respect of the 'lesser' barons. Another valuable source has been the 'Magna Carta Project' which provided details of King John's itinerary for the period 1214-1215.

As always specials thanks are due to Adele Fewings, for her enthusiastic administration and management of our website, to Roy Jackson for image design and to Glenis Summers for proof reading.

Andrew Summers
John Debenham

Glossary

Magna Carta, Great Charter, Charter, Articles of the Barons.
These are all basically the same. 'Magna Carta' is Latin for Great Charter. The term 'Magna Carta' did not come into regular use until 1217. The 'Articles of the Barons' was the first draft of the Magna Carta presented to the king at Runnymede in June 1215.

Barons. Powerful land holders representing the leading families and nobility of England. A baron was also called a Lord of the Manor. The barons sat on royal councils and were obliged to supply the king with men for military service when he demanded it. (see also scutage below)

Castellans. Royal Castle Governors.

Chevauchée. A term used to describe raiding in medieval warfare. Its purpose was to cause havoc and fear by burning and pillaging in the enemy countryside.

Crusades/Crusaders. The Crusades were military campaigns sanctioned by the Latin Roman Catholic Church with the stated goal of restoring Christian access to holy places in and near Jerusalem.

Justiciar. The chief minister in government, perhaps equivalent to a modern Prime Minister.

Motte-and-Bailey Castle. This is a fortification with a wooden or stone keep on a raised mound called the motte. Below is an enclosed courtyard, or bailey, surrounded by a protective ditch and palisade.

Papal Bull. A formal proclamation issued by the pope, so named after the Latin word for seal, 'Bulla'.

Parley. The parley (or negotiation) took place when the respective spokesmen of the besiegers (of castles) and the defenders rode out on horseback and met about half way between the battle lines to discuss the terms of surrender. If no agreement could be reached a siege began when the first shots were fired.

Saladin. Sultan of Egypt and Syria. Great warrior-leader of Muslim forces.

Saracens. In the middle ages the European name for Muslims, Arabs and followers of Saladin at the time of the Crusades.

Sénéchal. A royal officer (in France) charged with justice and the overall control of the administration in the land under his control.

Slighting. To raze or destroy (a fortification) to make it unusable for the enemy.

Miscellaneous General Terms

Darrein presentment. An action to determine who has the right to a position when two people are claiming it, particularly in relation to church livings.

Diffidatio. The act of renouncing allegiance, fealty and friendship to a lord or sovereign.

Disseisin. An action to recover lands of which the plaintiff had been disseised, or dispossessed. The action became extremely popular due to its expediency.

Fealty. A pledge of allegiance of one person to another as between the baron and the king.

Mort d'ancestor. An action brought where a plaintiff claimed the defendant had entered upon a freehold belonging to the plaintiff following the death of one of his relatives.

Scutage. A tax paid by barons in lieu of military service.

Courts and Officials

Court of Attachment or the Forty Day Court. A court held by the forest Verderers or Warden every forty days to assess crimes and take charge of suspects' property pending trial at Swanimote court.

Court of Regard. Court charged with the clawing of dogs.

Swanimote. Lower Forest Court of Verderers held three times annually with a jury of swains, or freemen of the forest.

Agistors. Court officials charged with calculating scales of charges and fines.

Sergeants or Forester in Fee. Men given small holdings in the forest by the crown. Their main duties were to seek out offenders. They were paid mainly on a commission basis.

Forester, Under-Foresters, Rangers. Forest Police Officers.

Justice in Eyre. A Circuit Judge that could sentence convicted offenders of the forest laws.

Reeve. Magistrate or official elected annually by the serfs to supervise lands for a lord.

Regarders. Officials charged with keeping detailed historic records of assarts, purpresture, waste and dogs kept by forest dwellers. (see below)

Verdereres. Lower tier justices of the forests especially at the Swanimote.

Forest terms

Amercements. Financial penalties.

Assart. The clearance of land to grow crops.

Chiminage. A toll paid by a traveller for passage through a forest.

Clawing or Expeditating. The act of removing claws from the front feet of a dog to prevent it from chasing deer and other forest animals.

Iter. The circuit travelled by the Justice in Eyre.

Pannage. Payments connected with the rights or privileges granted to local people to release domestic pigs on common land or in royal forests to feed on fallen acorns or other nuts.

Purpresture. The fencing off or wrongful enclosure of lands to the detriment of the vegetation (or vert) which rightfully ought to be open and free to the public at large.

Perambulation. The act of determining the bounds of a legal area by walking around it; particularly the boundaries of land subject to Forest Law when disafforestation was reducing the extent of the forest and the scope of forest law.

Principal Characters

King John of England was born in 1167 and died in 1216. He was the youngest son of Henry II and Eleanor of Aquitaine. On Henry's death in 1189, all of his lands were left to his eldest son, Richard I, better known as Richard the Lionheart. John, left with nothing, became known by the nick-name John Lackland. In 1199, Richard was killed in France and John became the king of England as well as inheriting all of Richard's French territories.

William the Marshal, or William Marshal, the 1st Earl of Pembroke, was born around 1146 and died in 1219. He was described by Stephen Langton, the Archbishop of Canterbury, as "the greatest knight who had ever lived". He served four kings – Henry II, Richard I, John, and Henry III. Marshall became regent of England when nine year old Henry III came to the throne and consequently was one of the most powerful men in Europe. William is credited with being the driving force behind the revival of the Magna Carta and restoring peace and order to England following the Barons' War of 1215/1217.

Prince Louis (later Louis VIII, the Lion, of France) was born in 1187 and died in 1226. He was the son of Philip II (of France) and Isabelle of Hainaut. Between 1215 and 1217 he claimed the English crown as the maternal grandson-in-law of the late English King Henry II. He was also invited by the rebel English barons to take the crown of England from King John. In May 1216, Louis invaded England in support of his claim and was proclaimed "King of England" in London on the 2nd June by the rebel forces. The rebels were subsequently defeated at the Battle of Lincoln in 1217. With his French supply fleet vanquished at the battle of Sandwich, Louis renounced all claim to England and, following the treaty of Lambeth, returned to France.

Henry III, King of England, the son of King John, was born in 1207 and died in 1272. Henry assumed the throne when he was only nine years of age and in the middle of the First Barons' War.

Pope Innocent III was born around 1160 and was pope from 1198 until his death in 1216. Pope Innocent claimed supremacy over all of Europe's kings. Though he excommunicated King John from 1209 to

1213, he supported his stand against the barons and declared the Magna Carta null and void following its sealing in 1215.

Stephen Langton was born in 1150 and died in 1228. He was appointed by Pope Innocent as Archbishop of Canterbury in 1207. A bitter dispute between King John and the pope followed which resulted in King John being excommunicated. The excommunication caused a crisis in England and the turmoil that resulted was one of the major factors leading to the creation of the Magna Carta in 1215.

Guala Bicchieri, simply known as Guala, was born in 1150 and died in 1227. He was an Italian diplomat and cardinal. He was the papal legate in England from 1216 to 1218. He played a prominent role, during King John's last years and in Henry III's early minority, in trying to reconcile the differences between the royalists and the rebels.

The **Essex Rebel Barons,** led by **Robert Fitzwalter,** Lord of Dunmow were; **Richard de Montfitchet**, Sheriff of Essex, **Geoffrey de Mandeville** of Pleshey, **William de Lanvallei,** the Governor of Colchester Castle, and **Robert de Vere** of Castle Hedingham. Details of these barons are covered in the following chapters. A northern rebel baron, also on the council of 25, was **John FitzRobert**, the Lord of Warkworth Castle in Northumberland. He was born around 1190 and died in 1240. His lands and titles included the castle and extensive lands around Clavering, south west of Saffron Walden.

Hubert de Burgh, the 1st Earl of Kent, was an ardent King John loyalist. He was born around 1160 and died around 1243. He was Justiciar of England and Ireland and one of the most influential men during the reigns of King John and of his infant son and successor King Henry III. De Burgh played a key role in the defence of Dover castle and commanded the English fleet which defeated the French at sea in the course of the Battle of Sandwich. Hubert de Burgh, who built Hadleigh Castle, had extensive land holdings encompassing Rayleigh, Hadleigh, Thundersley and Benfleet.

Savary de Mauléon was a French mercenary captain and adventurer who sided alternatively with King John and Philip II of France. De Mauléon was active in Essex during the Baron's War.

The Chroniclers

Much of what we know of the background and aftermath of the Magna Carta has come from contemporary chroniclers. Most were monks and nearly everything was written in Latin. Over the centuries the surviving chronicles have been translated and reinterpreted by leading historians of the day. Other sources exist, such as original official documents held in the National Archives at Kew or by the British Library. However, it is the Chronicles that bring the history of the Magna Carta to life, although it must be noted that the writers were not always unbiased.

Anonymous of Bethune chronicled the years 1185 to 1217. The works appeared sometime after 1220. They were compiled on behalf of Robert of Bethune (a Prince Louis loyalist) by a member of his entourage and detail the period from the perspective of Prince Louis and his commanders.

Matthew Paris lived between 1200 and 1259. A Benedictine monk at St Albans Abbey, he wrote a number of works in Latin, Anglo-Norman and some in French verse. They were mostly historical and were lavishly illustrated. His most important work was the *Chronica Majora*. Though only fifteen at the time of the Magna Carta he also contributed extensively to the '*Historia Anglorum'* which appeared 20 to 30 years later. He sympathized with the rebel cause and was a harsh critic of King John and Pope Innocent III.

Ralph of Coggeshall, birth date unknown, died in 1227. He was a monk and from 1207-18 the Abbot of the Cistercian Abbey at Coggeshall. He lived through the tumultuous events of the Magna Carta and much credence is given to his measured writings. He was a major contributor to the *Chronicon Anglicanum*. After he resigned as Abbot, due to ill health, Ralph continued to write until his death. He is believed to be buried somewhere in the grounds of Coggeshall Abbey.

Roger of Wendover, also a monk at St Albans Abbey, contributed extensively to the *Flores Historiarum* (Flowers of History). This work is especially valued for its detailed narrative of contemporary events such as the sealing of the Magna Carta and King John's ruthless raids in the English countryside. Roger died in May 1236.

Excommunication

Excommunication, in simple terms, means exclusion from participation in the sacraments and services of the Christian Church. In the lead up to the Magna Carta it had great relevance. It is the severest censure that the Church can inflict and deprives the recipient of all participation in the common blessings of church society. When it happened to King John, his subjects were absolved from their oaths of allegiance. It gave the Barons reason to revolt and allowed the King of France the right to invade England to remove John from power. The consequences for the whole country could have been dire indeed.

Between 1209 and 1213, King John was excommunicated for his refusal to accept the pope's nominee, Stephen Langton, as Archbishop of Canterbury; the King wanted John de Grey, Bishop of Norwich. In the pope's view all kings were subservient to him in spiritual matters and he was determined to have his way.

An interdict issued prior to John's excommunication barred English priests from holding religious services except for baptisms and confessions. For a deeply religious England, banning church marriages or burials was catastrophic. This sanction, which lasted until the excommunication was lifted, specifically hurt the baronial classes. They could not legally marry in church and on death the best they could expect was the equivalent to a cheap pauper's burial. No longer was a grand plot and headstone in the churchyard available, nor was there the opportunity to erect a bust or other memorial within the confines of the church.

After nearly four years, John relented under pressure; the pope had won, Stephen Langton was Archbishop of Canterbury. Though the excommunication was lifted the price was high. John's letter of concession to the pope offered a large annual cash sum and made England a fiefdom of Rome. The terms of the concession were draconian too in that if the conditions were not met the Crown of England would be surrendered to the Roman Catholic Church forever.

In medieval Europe, though excommunication was a matter of spirituality, it had as much to do with the wielding of power and coming to agreeable business arrangements.

Kings and Barons

For sixteen years, firstly under King Richard I (the Lionheart) and then King John, the English, together with other European states, at the behest of the Catholic Church and successive popes, had been seeking to drive Saladin's forces out of the Holy Land. A new crusade (the third) had been called in 1187 by Pope Gregory VIII; its purpose was to retake Jerusalem in the name of Christianity.

Richard became King of England in 1189 and almost immediately set out on the crusade. Whilst returning overland from the Middle East, he was captured near Vienna and held prisoner by the Emperor of Germany in Dürnstein Castle overlooking the River Danube. Three years later he was released but only after a substantial ransom had been paid.

Not only King of England, Richard was also Duke of Aquitaine and his main home was in France with his mother Eleanor of Aquitaine. Although he reigned over England for ten years, he spoke only French and spent barely six months in England. He died, aged 41, after being hit by an arrow from a crossbow during a siege in Chalus, France.

Under England's complicated, and often disputed, laws of Royal succession, Arthur, the grandson of Henry II, Richard's father, was the designated heir to the throne of England, in preference to John, Richard's brother. John, it was well known, resented this and craved to be king believing that it was his right.

On Richard's departure to the crusade, John was given extensive lands in England, on condition that he stayed out of the country for three years. This was to stop him making mischief; it was thought that in three years Richard would be back. However, John returned after only two years to begin undermining the authority of Richard's administrators who were running the country. Before long armed conflicts broke out between John's supporters and those of the king and he was banished again. Whilst absent this time John set about forging alliances with the French, even claiming that Richard had died in captivity.

After Richard's release the brothers were somehow reconciled and on his death bed Richard forgave all and, believing Arthur too young to be king at the age of twelve, decreed John as his successor.

John was duly crowned at Westminster Abbey on 27th May 1199. The following year John annulled his marriage to Isabel the Countess of Gloucester. He chose a new wife, Isabella of Angoulême. This provoked a new war with the French King as Isabella was promised to someone else. The war went badly and by 1206 John had lost many of his French possessions. These failures were a damaging blow to his prestige. Yet, one piece of good news, at least as far as John was concerned, was that during the conflict Arthur (his rival to the throne) was imprisoned in Rouen Castle, where he subsequently vanished under mysterious circumstances. Whether John had a hand in it remains unclear.

Although King John was not very interested in crusading (John didn't confess this to the pope) he was determined to win back his hereditary lands in France. This required money, lots of money, so his government became increasingly ruthless and efficient in its financial administration. As John's reign progressed, taxes soared and he began to exploit his feudal rights ever more harshly. Under feudal law the nobility of England were obliged to supply men, armour, horses, livestock and all manner of supplies for the crown. Yet the king's wars of territorial conquest in France were becoming increasingly expensive and had no end in sight. There was an alternative for the nobility. They could buy themselves out of their military service obligations for a fee known as *scutage*. This revenue stream enabled the king to hire mercenaries to fight his battles. Yet the wars went on and the demands of the king continued to grow. The situation was becoming intolerable and bred increasing baronial discontent.

King John was seen by many as a man not to be trusted. He was adept at changing sides as the wind blew. He had a reputation for seducing other men's wives and drew little distinction between the women from the nobility or peasantry. His duplicitous dealings during Richard's crusade and imprisonment were still well remembered and Arthur's disappearance at Rouen still cast a shadow. For a time King John was even excommunicated (see page 21) by the Pope which increased baronial disaffection further.

Many of the English barons now believed that the resources of England were simply being used as a revenue stream to be squandered in the king's foreign adventures. The previous English kings, Richard and Henry II, had spent most of their reigns abroad so had largely left the barons alone. However John spent most of his time in England and personally oversaw all revenue raising matters.

In the summer of 1213, King John's excommunication was formally lifted but the price was high. In return the king received papal blessing for his numerous territorial claims in France. As a consequence the English barons, who had little interest in helping the king to regain his disputed French lands, saw their authority further undermined. Now they were obliged to support whatever reckless schemes the king embarked upon, since whatever he chose to do in pursuit of his claims came with the pope's authority.

Dürnstein Castle above the River Danube where Richard the Lionheart was imprisoned for three years.

The English Countryside 1215

Whilst the barons may have felt more and more disgruntled under King John's rule, it was nothing compared to the ruthlessness of law enforcement exercised in the countryside.

England in 1215 had a population of approximately four million, about the same size as today's Essex plus the five east London Boroughs formerly in the county. Ninety percent of the very rural population lived and worked on land owned by the other ten per cent. Some, on small tenanted farms, scraped a living from their crops plus the few animals they kept. For most it was at best a meagre subsistence; but a way of life that had existed for generations.

As the king's demands on the barons grew they naturally sought to recoup their losses elsewhere. New burdens fell upon tenant farmers and their dependants. There had been a steep rise in inflation in the early years of John's reign, which apart from significantly raising prices had also led to a new class of professional revenue collectors who were often only paid by results. For example, County Sheriff positions could be bought. The position had no regular salary but a considerable income could be obtained by 'persuading' hapless tenants to pay more for leases and rents and from the collection of a host of taxes and levies which either already existed or had been newly introduced.

Maximising tax collection meant giving the collectors power. To this end, King John authorised the engagement of many of the mercenaries that supported his failed French campaigns. These included several of his former military captains. Once again little or no salary was offered but the pickings were rich. These men had the right sort of skills to clamp down on any form of non-payment or suggestion of rebellion and they used them without mercy. As a consequence, in the space of a few years John had managed to transform the norms of government from reluctant acceptance into a resented and hated tyranny.

No one ever liked paying taxes and royal officers were always viewed with a degree of suspicion and fear but this new band of heavy handed foreign enforcers united the peasantry, landowners and nobility in opposition as never before.

The Great Forest of Essex

In the year 1215, when the Magna Carta was sealed, the whole county of Essex was designated 'Forest'. The word forest comes from the Latin forestis meaning outside. Forest did not simply mean an area of densely wooded oak and beech, picturesque glades and clearings such as Epping Forest is today. The medieval 'Forest' was an area of unenclosed countryside. Forest land could be part wooded, part agricultural with meadows where livestock grazed, just plain heath or scrub land and could even include towns and villages.

Significantly, 'Forest' was also an area where 'Forest Laws' applied. These were laws separate and distinct from those of the central administration and the common law. All who lived and worked in the forest were subject to the 'Forest Laws', which were superior to the laws of all other courts of the land.

This concept of 'Forest' was established by the Normans following the invasion of 1066. Initially the sole purpose of areas designated 'Forest' was that they would be used as exclusive game reserves for hunting by royalty and their supporters. William the Conqueror and his sons were famed for their devotion to hunting. Deer and other game needed a variety of habitats — thick woodland so that the animals could rest and hide in daylight and more open land for feeding at night.

In the 150 years from the time of the Normans the 'forest' concept was enthusiastically maintained and extended by successive monarchs. By 1215 approximately one third of England, twenty-nine counties including Essex, were forested to a greater or lesser degree. The forest had become much more than a simple royal game reserve. Forest resources and the zealous application of 'Forest Law' was one of the most profitable ways to raise money for the crown.

For the people who lived and worked within forest bounds, 'Forest Law' had little to do with justice. They saw it as just another way to tax them. Everybody was subject to a complex set of regulations, implemented by royal officials who were answerable only to the king. The king's rule was arbitrary and his word was final and could not be challenged by other courts in the land. The king could designate which areas of the country could be forest on a whim and extend them at will.

Henry II was fanatical about hunting and he greatly extended the area of forest in England. Although his son, Richard I, was hardly ever in the country the forest lands were extended under his reign too. King John was not an enthusiastic hunter but the application of 'Forest Law' with its lucrative revenue stream was his priority. Accordingly he did whatever he could to make further extensions.

Over the years the scope of Forest Law grew impressively through a bewildering labyrinth of courts and officials. Initially no-one other than royalty was allowed to hunt deer or game within the forest boundaries. Culprits, if caught stalking the king's game, could have their hands cut off or be blinded. New rules were then added to impose penalties for anyone disturbing the wildlife or the environment they lived in. Restrictions were placed on forest dwellers in regard to what animals they could keep and how they were fed. For land owners the clearance of land on their own property incurred a fee if they had permission from the king and a fine plus a fee as well if no royal authority had been granted. The laws even applied to neighbouring land owners who lived outside the forest. They could be charged with disturbing the forest and lived under the constant threat that the king could arbitrarily designate their land as forest.

A whole new vocabulary came into use. Forest dwellers regularly suffered amercements (financial penalties) for such things as carrying out assarts (clearance of the land to grow crops) and purpresture (fencing off land where it might harm the existing vegetation or vert). A whole set of regulations, along with a schedule of payments and fines, governed the disposal of waste (wood and vegetation) created from land clearance. Anyone who kept a dog had to have it clawed or expeditated (the dog had to have its fore feet mutilated) in order to discourage it from chasing deer. Greyhounds could not be kept except by special warrant. There were payments (pannage) connected to the grazing of livestock, especially pigs, on forest land. Added to this there were strict rules about who kept bows and arrows, cross-bows and even nets. Naturally all who broke rules were fined. If the offence happened on a freeholder's property, the land would pass into the king's hands until the fine was paid.

To enforce the 'forest laws' special courts were set up. The primary court of the forest was the Court of Attachment, later called the Forty Day Court. The lower court was the Swanimote, overseen by a Chief Warden and run by the freeholders living in the forest. Offenders were summoned or brought before the Swanimote where the evidence was heard and guilt determined. However, sentencing was left to the travelling justices (known as Justices in Eyre) during their circuit (or Iter). Additionally, the Court of Regard was held every third year to enforce the law requiring declawing of dogs within the forest.

The imposition of the 'Forest Laws' and the staffing of the courts was the responsibility of a multitude of officials. The Chief Royal Official was the Warden, usually a local member of the nobility. The policing of the forest was exacted though foresters and under-foresters, later called rangers. Their prime responsibility was to seek out and apprehend offenders.

In court Verderers* acted as lower tier justices, often with assistance from the Reeve (Magistrate). Court officials included the Regarders, charged with keeping detailed historic records of assarts, purpresture, waste and the declawing of dogs.

Other court appointees were Agistors whose duties included working out how much should be paid in charges for pannage and other fees relating to grazing rights and sale of waste etc. Perhaps more sinister were the Sergeants or Foresters-in-Fee, men given small holdings in the forest. These were supposedly crown paid positions, but rarely was a salary paid. Instead the men were supposed to 'live off the land' and derive bounty from apprehending offenders.

*Verderers *Although the term dropped out of use for 200 years there are four Verderers who sit on the committee that manages Epping Forest today. They are voluntary, unpaid positions but expert in forest matters. As far as we know they have no powers to exact summary justice!*

King John, desperately needing money, determined to extract the maximum out of the forest. 'Forest Law' became widely abused and open to corruption. Despite this, the threat of cutting off an offender's hands or blinding them if they were caught hunting wild animals was rarely carried out. There was no profit in maiming someone. If the crime was repeated more fines could be levied and, depending on the status of the offender, he or she could be pressed into some form of service.

The unimpeded growth of the forest in King John's reign produced real grievances all around. Extensions absorbed neighbouring manors on an arbitrary basis. Lords of manors within the forest were not allowed to convert their land from pasture into arable, nor could they cut down their woods, or put up fencing or make any enclosures to prevent forest animals or vermin eating crops. Fencing also interfered with the royal huntsmen's rights to chase their prey freely in the forest and they thought little of riding roughshod over cultivated gardens.

The severity of the Forest Laws and the intolerable hardships inflicted, united both Lords and forest dwellers as never before in opposition to the king. It is therefore not surprising that five Essex barons were in the forefront of opposition to King John.

The 'Forest' has been a rich source down the ages for sensational writing, especially in reference to the Norman and Saxon divide. It was from the chaos and banditry of the time just before John became king, or during his early reign, that the legend of *Robin Hood* was born.

There is a legend that Maid Marion (of Robin Hood fame) was the daughter of the leader of the Magna Carta barons, Robert Fitzwalter (the Lord of Dunmow). Matthew Paris, in the 13th century, wrote in his diary; 'FitzWalter had a daughter, Matilda the Fair, called 'Maid Marion,' said to have been poisoned by King John'.

The legend has it that Matilda (Marion) married Robin Earl of Huntingdon (Robin Hood) after rejecting the advances of King John. John, not one to accept rejection, allegedly poisoned Matilda (Marion) by sending her a poisoned bracelet which killed her. Marion, or Matilda, is buried in the Priory Church in Little Dunmow in Essex.

Image of Matilda daughter of Robert Fitzwater.
Matilda was perhaps confused with Maid Marion.

Tipping Point

As we have seen in previous chapters dissatisfaction had been building up with King John's rule for some time. Apart from his dwindling band of loyalists, support for the king was fast ebbing away. English nobility, represented by a number of powerful barons, began to form a credible opposition, not just in a political sense, but they also began to refuse to pay their scutage and even pledged to resort to armed conflict. By early 1215 it was estimated that two thirds of the barons had abandoned the king. One of the most critical barons was Robert Fitzwalter, Lord of Dunmow, who proclaimed himself *Marshal of the Army of God and the Holy Church*. He had already been exiled once by King John for plotting against him.

There were a number of key events that brought King John to Runnymede. In Excommunication (see page 21) we saw that King John returned to the papal fold by promising to pay the Vatican in Rome a huge annual cash sum (which neither he nor the country could actually afford). More alarmingly for English people, as part of the agreement for lifting the excommunication, the king agreed to surrender England's sovereignty to the pope, essentially a 'foreign' power. On 15th May 1213, John presided over a lavish ceremony, witnessed by nearly all of the English baronage, to confirm the handover. One crumb of comfort for the nobility was that Robert Fitzwalter was allowed to return from exile.

Once the ceremony was over, the king showed his darker side. He celebrated by ordering the execution of Peter of Wakefield (and his son). Peter of Wakefield, an illiterate wandering hermit, had predicted the downfall of King John by 1213. He had attracted a widespread following and his words had even spread to France. John originally had Peter locked up. Once the papal handover was confirmed he felt able get rid of this irritant once and for all.

King John, despite increasing baronial misgivings, now felt free to pursue his territorial claims in France with renewed vigour. Initially, naval success came when English ships and their allies succeeded in destroying a large French fleet off Flanders on what is now the Belgian coast. This military triumph and the plunder acquired not only topped up the Royal coffers; it also boosted John's confidence and emboldened him to plan a large French invasion.

In February 1214, a two pronged assault on the French mainland took place. King John, at the head of his army, landed on the French Atlantic coast near the port of La Rochelle with the intention of driving east and north. Another army, led by William Longsword, King John's half-brother, crossed the channel to northern France where they hoped to link up with Otto IV of Germany, an English ally, and then drive south and west. On paper the plan was sound. Its aim was to divide the French forces of King Philip and pick them off one by one.

At La Rochelle there was no French Army of any consequence for the English to face. The king dithered and began to waste precious time and money bribing local magnates for support and making extravagant promises of land grants that he couldn't possibly keep. Despite this, during the spring and early summer of 1214, John's army made some territorial headway. At the town of Angers in the River Loire Valley, 130 miles from La Rochelle, Prince Louis (King Philip's son) mustered his forces to confront the English. However, rather than engaging the enemy, John's forces hastily retreated in disarray. All hope of support from the magnates he had bribed evaporated as they too refused to fight or simply changed allegiance.

Meanwhile on 27th July 1214, in northern France, near Lille, William Longsword's army met with disaster at the battle of Bouvines. The English were comprehensively routed and Longsword was taken prisoner by the French. King Philip, victorious, was free to join his son and drive the English out. King John had no choice but to sue for terms. A five year peace deal was agreed with the French that cost another fortune in cash, but nevertheless allowed John to safely leave France.

King John returned to England utterly defeated. His French sortie had emptied the Royal treasury. Now, more than ever, he had to come to terms with the increasingly resentful English nobility. In the words of the medieval historian and Magna Carta expert, the late Sir James Holt, "The road from Bouvines to Runnymede was direct, short and unavoidable".

The Road to Runnymede

"The road from Bouvines to Runnymede was direct, short and unavoidable." Indeed it was! The French defeat of English forces in July 1214 at the Battle of Bouvines was the last of King John's disastrous French campaign. In October he returned, near bankrupt, to find England on the verge of revolution. In January 1215 the king met a group of disaffected barons in London. Most of them were in little mood for compromise and full blown rebellion was in the air. The barons demanded, as a minimum, the restoration of the ancient liberties granted by Henry I one hundred years previously. John, in reply, aggravated the barons even further by demanding immediate payment of any outstanding *scutage* (tax in lieu of service).

It was a game of high stakes with the future of the king and the rights of his people in the balance. If the king was in trouble, the barons were in a difficult position too. Previous rebellions had always focused on rival claims to the throne or disputes about royal succession. The seeds of this rebellion were different; its purpose was to tame the worst excesses of the king. Above all it was a rebellion about rights. All previous kings, once enthroned, believed they had a divine right to rule absolutely and King John was no exception. He believed it was his right to claim scutage, plus any other taxes he deemed necessary, as well as to have the unswerving loyalty of his subjects no matter what. In this John had papal backing, having already acknowledged the pope as his feudal lord.

The January meeting ended without agreement. John promised to take the barons' proposals and consider them. He hastily dispatched emissaries to Rome to advise Pope Innocent III of his situation, urging him to condemn anyone who defied 'an obedient son of the church' (i.e. himself). At the same time he also prepared for civil war by putting all his trusted castellans (Royal Castle Governors) on a state of high alert. The king's opponents, the barons, who had sworn an oath to stand together for the liberty of the church and the realm, also sent emissaries to Rome seeking papal support. Another meeting was arranged for the end of April 1215.

The king was playing for time. When the pope's reply came it was just what John had hoped for. The pope asked him to listen to any legitimate grievances raised by his subjects; condemned absolutely any council or league that threatened his right to rule and ordered the barons to pay all outstanding taxes. John took this to show that the pope was his staunch ally in upholding his right to rule.

Despite threats from both the king and the pope, the idea of a charter of liberties was gaining momentum. Then, to the amazement of the rebels, King John promised Rome that he would take part in another crusade. Writing to the pope he declared that anyone opposing him was worse than a Saracen (see glossary). This attempt to curry favour fooled no one, the king was broke and the rebels knew it. At the scheduled meeting in April the barons met. Prominent among them were Robert Fitzwalter Lord of Dunmow, the king's old adversary, and Geoffrey de Mandeville the Earl of Essex, whose principal manorial seat was at Pleshey Castle. The king however did not attend.

On 5th May 1215 the barons formally renounced their allegiance to King John. Civil war was inevitable. From this point events moved rapidly. The rebel forces, led by Robert Fiztwalter, moved south and occupied London. This was a significant victory. John had tried to pacify Londoners with a sudden offer to restore their liberties, reduce taxation and allow them to elect a mayor. However the offer, seen as a blatant bribe, had come too late and Londoners remained firmly within the rebel cause.

The king's position was becoming more hopeless by the day. He desperately needed to gain more time to build up his forces to oppose the rebels but in order to do that he had to make a significant concession. During May and early June envoys scuttled back and forth between the rebels' headquarters in London and King John, ensconced in Windsor Castle. Documents setting out peace proposals were drafted, redrafted and argued over. The Archbishop of Canterbury, Stephen Langton, even acted as a mediator.

John met the rebel leaders face to face on the 10th June 1215. He was presented with a draft of demands for reform known as *The Articles of the Barons.*

The journey to Runnymede was complete.

June 1215

The fifteenth of June 1215 has acquired mythical status as the date the Magna Carta was signed at Runnymede. The myth contains a number of misconceptions. The date itself is uncertain; it may have been on 16th, 17th or 18th June, also King John didn't sign anything. His great seal was affixed, in all probability by one of his clerks, to the bottom of a lengthy document, called *The Articles of the Barons*. The seal was proof of the king's assent. The name Magna Carta, the Latin for Great Charter, only came into being two years later when it was the name given to a modified version of the original document.

King John was certainly literate, well educated by the standards of the day and had access to the royal library. Whether he actually wrote anything is unknown. He didn't need to; he had scribes to do that for him. Writing in 1215, in the absence of keyboards or modern pens, was a messy business. In any event legal documents were made official by seals, not by signatures. The document sealed at Runnymede was only the first draft. It took nearly another month for the final copies to be ready for delivery throughout England. Each handwritten copy of the charter, with the king's great seal attached, was by all accounts a work of art. Only four of these original copies survive today, one in Lincoln Cathedral, one in Salisbury Cathedral and two at the British Library. The only copy still having the great seal affixed to it is one of those kept in the British Library. Unfortunately it was damaged in a fire and is only partially readable. A copy of the *Articles of the Barons*, crafted for 15th June 1215, can also be seen in the British Library.

On the 19th June, with the charter agreed, most of the rebel barons renewed their oaths of loyalty to King John and departed. However, a significant minority of them had left early, refusing to agree. The fact that many of them had retained their forces in a state of readiness indicated that the settlement was destined to be short lived.

There were two clauses in the *Articles of the Barons* that King John would seem to have been most aggrieved about numbers 61 and 52. Clause 61 runs to over 500 words in its modern English translation. In essence it allowed for the setting up of a council of twenty five barons (selected by the rebels themselves) charged with ensuring the king and all his royal officials adhered to the terms of the charter. It also allowed the barons collectively to take all necessary actions to correct any royal transgressions.

Clause 52 reads:- *To any man whom we have deprived or dispossessed of lands, castles, liberties, or rights, without the lawful judgment of his equals, we will at once restore these. In cases of dispute the matter shall be resolved by the judgment of the twenty-five barons referred to below in the clause for securing the peace.*

Its implications for royalty are quite clear. The king was no longer sole arbiter of disputes. Clause 52 even made it possible that royal lands could be confiscated if so ordered by the barons. Already there were simmering disputes centred on demands for the return of lands previously acquired by the king or his supporters. King John now felt he was no longer the absolute king in England. His status had been relegated to that of just another overlord like the 25 barons. This was unacceptable for a medieval monarch.

The 25 barons selected for the new council were all rebels. Five had manorial seats in Essex. Many among the rebels found excuses to keep their forces mobilised. Above all the barons refused to surrender to the king the city of London, which they controlled, until the charter had been fully implemented. Meanwhile King John began raising an army of mercenaries. He also sent messengers to the pope requesting that the charter be annulled.

The *Articles of the Barons* had begun life as a demand for the rights of free men, in particular the barons. It was something for everyone, except serfs and tied or 'unfree' labour. It demanded protection of church rights, swift access to justice, safeguards from unjust imprisonment and limitations on taxation. It also proposed that the king be subject to the law. The document was intended to be the basis for a peace agreement between the king and his subjects. Yet it was so heavily weighted in the rebels' favour it had little chance of surviving.

Clauses 52 and 61 turned what we know as the Magna Carta, which began as a peace treaty, into a recipe for war. Such was the distrust between the two parties that, within three months, war is just what ensued.

War

Pope Innocent III, in Rome, read King John's communications about the terms of the Magna Carta with growing alarm. In England rebels were in control of London and refused to surrender.

On 24th August 1215, the pope issued a proclamation known as a Papal bull. The bull declared that the charter was "illegal, unjust, harmful to royal rights and shameful to the English people – it was null and void of all validity for ever". The pope also added that the charter compromised his rights as King John's feudal lord. The English king had been forced to agree under duress which was outrageous. In addition, the rebel barons were excommunicated. In another move the Archbishop of Canterbury, Steven Langton, was suspended. Although he had originally been nominated by Pope Innocent, Langton was, quite rightly it would transpire, suspected of siding with the rebels.

Less than three months after the council at Runnymede the barons concluded that peace with King John was impossible. They had also sent messages to the pope offering to tear up the charter but these had been ignored. The Magna Carta was effectively dead. Allegiance to the king was withdrawn but once more the rebels had to tread carefully. There were misgivings within their ranks as to the enormity of what they had done. The more militant barons, however, were adamant that threats from the pope should be ignored; further negotiation was useless and the only way to succeed was by using force. Their view prevailed. What was known as the First Barons' War had begun. They called on Philip II of France's son, the future Louis VIII, for help. Louis, as a maternal grandson-in-law of English King Henry II, claimed the English throne for himself.

London remained the rebel headquarters. From there the rebels struck out first. The leader of the Council of Twenty-Five, Robert Fitzwalter, Lord of Dunmow and self-proclaimed *Marshal of the Army of God and Holy Church*, sent a force to Rochester Castle, one of the strongest castles in Kent. Within the city of Rochester, it came under the jurisdiction of the diocese of Canterbury and therefore Steven Langton.

Fitzwalter's 'Army' approached the Castle gates and demanded entry which was granted. The rebels took over, immediately installing their own garrison. Their plan was for Rochester Castle to serve as a bastion to keep the king's forces tied up until Prince Louis and his French reinforcements arrived in England.

King John was outraged that the castle was given up with hardly a fight. In October 1215 he counter attacked and laid siege to Rochester. The town fell almost immediately. For the defenders in the castle there was no sign of the promised French reinforcements. Seven weeks later, on 30th November, the starving survivors within the keep yielded and the castle fell. John had shown remarkable determination, some spirited leadership and an uncharacteristic degree of mercy to the men who surrendered.

Whilst the king had been detained in Kent, his enemies were making the most of the situation in the rest of the country. In December several thousand Frenchmen landed and made their way to London. After the fall of Rochester Castle and with London still occupied by rebel forces, King John convened a conference of royalist supporters at St Albans. His plan involved dividing his forces into two armies. He left an army of loyalists in the south to contain the situation in London and then headed to Nottingham to attack the estates of the rebel northern barons. John travelled as far north as Scotland. He laid waste to all before him in a reign of terror wherever he encountered resistance.

In January 1216 he attacked Alexander II of Scotland, who had allied himself with the rebel cause, and captured Berwick, then Scotland's largest town. From there he launched raids into the Scottish lowlands before turning his attention south again. On his departure Berwick was burnt to the ground.

For three months the king's forces had held the military initiative. Where he had faced opposition the rebels had either fled or submitted. However the government of England had broken down. The treasury was bankrupt. John's army was no more than a marauding band living off the land. Yet for the rebels there was still no sign of Prince Louis' promised major force from France.

The war had settled into a stalemate.

The King's Mercenary

John's army in the south was under the overall command of his half-brother William Longsword, the Earl of Salisbury. Their task was to prevent any possible breakout from the capital and to subdue unrest in East Anglia.

Most of John's fighting men were French Mercenaries. One of their captains was Savary de Mauléon, or Savaricius de Maleone. He was a French nobleman and a soldier of fortune who supported Arthur, Duke of Brittany's claim to the English Crown (see page 22). Captured at the battle of Mirebeau in 1202, he was imprisoned by King John in Corfe Castle, Dorset. Two years later, John forgave him and named him as his Seneschal* of Poitou in France. In 1212 Philip II of France 'bought' his services and de Mauléon switched sides. He was given command of a large fleet with which to invade England. However, during the 30th and 31st May 1213, the fleet, moored in the harbour of Damme (near present day Bruges), was comprehensively destroyed by the English in a pre-emptive strike. De Mauléon survived the raid and switched sides yet again to return to England with King John. He was one of the king's witnesses when the Magna Carta was sealed at Runnymede and was with John during the seven week siege of Rochester Castle.

With the king away campaigning in the north there was little for de Mauléon to do. London, firmly under rebel control, was well supplied and securely defended. There was no sign of a breakout. It was impossible to starve London into submission and the royalist forces were not strong enough to mount an all-out assault. For all intents and purposes London was impregnable.

William Longsword directed his mercenaries, under the captaincy of de Mauléon, to turn their attentions to East Anglia. Essex and Suffolk offered rich pickings. Most of the castles, manors and estates, with the exception Rayleigh Castle (controlled by Hubert de Burgh the King's Chief Justiciar or Chief Minister), were in the hands of rebel barons.

Sénéchal A royal officer charged with justice and the overall control of the administration in the land under his control.

In late December 1215, Savary de Mauléon gathered his men together and headed east on a series of *chevauchées*. *Chevauchée* was a particularly savage aspect of medieval warfare. It caused fear and havoc by burning, pillaging and laying waste to the countryside.

Mountfitchet Castle (close to present day Stansted airport), a Norman style Motte and Bailey castle, was a short distance from London. As the seat of Richard de Montfichet, who was firmly in the rebel camp, it was an obvious target. In 1214, at the age of twenty, Montfichet had fought with King John at Poitou. A year later he had joined the rebels and was chosen to be one of the twenty five barons charged with enforcing the terms of the Magna Carta. As part of the Runnymede settlement large areas of 'Mountfichet ancestral forest', previously confiscated by the crown, had been restored to him.

Details of what actually happened when Mountfitchet Castle was attacked are sketchy and conflicting. A possible scenario is that following an ultimatum from Savary de Mauléon, whose mercenaries vastly outnumbered Mountfichet's garrison, the defenders surrendered or fled. The mercenaries then proceeded to ransack the castle and lay waste the surrounding village. After taking whatever booty they could lay their hands on, they destroyed everything possible and any buildings still standing were torched before the army moved on. Luckily for young Richard de Montfitchet, he was absent during the raid, probably in London.

With the castle in ruins, their feudal overlord gone and the garrison dispersed, local villagers then took the opportunity to do a spot of looting of their own. Much of what remained within the confines of the castle that was salvageable, even the very stones, was removed and used to rebuild the village. The castle was never rebuilt as a defensive installation The 'castle' that stands on the site today was constructed in the late 20th century as a 'replica' of the original Norman structure and serves as a tourist attraction.

It would seem strange that Richard de Montfitchet should be a prominent member of the rebels. He was made a royal ward on his father's death, being only 10 years old, and then, at 19 or 20, he showed his loyalty to King John by fighting with him at Poitou. Was he persuaded to join the rebels by close family ties? He was related to the baronial leaders Robert Fitzwalter and Richard, Earl of Clare, who had also served on King John's expedition to Poitou. Or did he join the barons, perhaps in the hope, successful as it turned out, of recovering the forestry rights forfeited by his family under Henry II?

Whatever the reasons, Montfitchet's lands were confiscated and he remained fighting the rebel cause until after John's death. He fought at the battle of Lincoln where he was captured and imprisoned by Henry III's forces but later made peace with Henry and all his lands were restored to him.

The next target for the mercenaries lay 15 miles east at Pleshey. Pleshey Castle was also in rebel hands. It was the seat of Geoffrey de Mandeville, one time Earl of Essex and another of the Essex barons on the council of twenty five.

Contemporary chronicles record that on Christmas Eve 1215 Pleshey Castle was attacked. There is no mention of Geoffrey de Mandeville and it is assumed he too was absent when the king's forces arrived. Nevertheless his castle was taken and all his lands promptly confiscated.

The next day, Christmas Day, some of the mercenaries left Pleshey to march about twelve miles north to the Cistercian Abbey at Tilty, between Dunmow and Thaxted. The chronicler Ralph of Coggeshall recorded:-

On Christmas Day 1215 King John's soldiers attacked the abbey and broke into the church while Christmas mass was being said. The soldiers ransacked the church, broke into chests and carried off anything of value.

Either as a result of the attack, or shortly after, several monks were killed. Little remains of the abbey. Like nearly all other monasteries in England it was demolished during the reign of Henry VIII. Despite the destruction, the grave slabs of two of the slain monks were recovered and placed within the Parish Church of Tilty, St Mary the Virgin. Presently the slabs are set upright on the north wall of the sanctuary. It is not now possible to read the individual monks' names on the worn stone. Yet 800 years later they serve as a reminder of the dreadful attack.

After a few days rest within the relative comfort of Pleshey Castle, Savary de Mauléon moved his forces twenty miles further east to Coggeshall and another Cistercian abbey. Ralph of Coggeshall, the historian and serving 6th Abbott, contributed to the medieval narrative the *Chronicon Anglicanum*, an extract of which tersely states:-

On New Year's Day (1216) at Coggeshall, while the third hour was said, they violently entered the church and led away twenty two horses which were the property of the Bishop of London.

On this occasion no deaths were reported. After the raid on Coggeshall, de Mauléon's troops marched into Suffolk towards Bury St Edmonds, creating havoc and destruction as they went. Such was the fear they created with their 'scorched earth' policy, most of the people fled the town. Refugees, known supporters or sympathizers to the barons' cause, were pursued over frozen ground towards Ely in Cambridgeshire, where maybe they sought sanctuary in the great cathedral. Ralph of Coggeshall again describes the events at Ely in graphic terms,

They (the king's men) made great slaughter, sparing neither age, nor sex, nor the clergy.

Another chronicler wrote of scenes of utter devastation where the king's enemies were imprisoned, tortured, put in chains and made to pay heavy ransoms. Towns, churches and even cemeteries were robbed or desecrated with livestock being stolen or killed.

De Mauléon's next move was to return to Essex and Colchester. Colchester Castle had been granted to the Lanvallei family by King Richard I about thirty years before the sealing of the Magna Carta.

The preceding year, in November 1214, King John had been in Colchester and had stayed in the castle for two days. The king was already at odds with much of the nobility of England and William de Lanvallei was no exception. John left Colchester and travelled to Rayleigh Castle in the south of the county arriving on the 7th November. There he presumably conferred with his justicar Hubert de Burgh and issued a writ commanding the surrender of Colchester Castle. It was placed in the hands of Stephen Harengood, one of the king's trusted henchmen, who installed his own garrison and upgraded the castle's defences. Despite this loss, de Lanvallei, even though he too had served with King John at Poitou, remained more committed to the rebels than ever. He was also one of the 25 barons charged with enforcing the terms of the charter and, like Richard de Montfitchet, his family was related to both Robert Fitzwalter and Geoffrey de Mandeville. When the charter was agreed at Runnymede on June 15th, as part of the settlement, Colchester Castle was restored to its hereditary owner William de Lanvallei. Lanvallei wasted no time in putting his own men in and further strengthening the castle defences. The garrison was also reinforced by a French contingent loyal to the rebel cause.

The king's army, led by Savary de Mauléon, arrived in Colchester in late January 1216. Colchester, however, was unlike the lightly defended Montfitchet or Pleshey castles or the easy pickings at Tilty, Coggeshall and Bury St Edmonds. Colchester was a substantial stone built castle that was heavily fortified. The garrison was well supplied and determined to keep the stronghold. De Mauléon inspected the castle and issued some threats. A few half-hearted sorties were made to test the defences but these were easily brushed off by the soldiers manning the castle walls. Eventually de Mauléon came to the conclusion that attempting to take Colchester Castle with the forces at his disposal was not going to be possible. There were also rumours that a large relief force was on its way from London. For a few days he created havoc in the town of Colchester itself before moving off to rendezvous with King John who was travelling south from battling with the northern barons.

Savary de Mauléon remained loyal to King John throughout his reign. On his deathbed in 1216, King John nominated de Mauléon to serve on the Council of Regency headed by William Marshall to govern England in the name of nine year old King Henry III. In about 1220 Henry III re-appointed de Mauléon as *Sénéchal* of Poitou, France.

Poitou and the area around La Rochelle were still subject to conflict as part of the ongoing rival territorial claims between the English and French monarchs. In 1224, the port of La Rochelle and the adjacent coast fell to the French. The English immediately accused Savary de Mauléon of surrendering the port too easily. Perhaps he had switched sides yet again having received a better offer? There is little in England to remember de Mauléon. He died in 1233. Curiously, despite his warlike tendencies, he gained a reputation as a poet. In France he is described as the *Prince Poète* of the XIII century. Just north of La Rochelle is the prestigious educational establishment, the *Lycée Savary De Mauléon*.

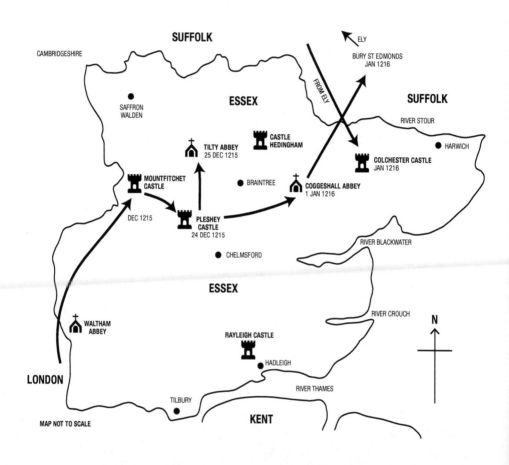

*Probable route of Savary de Mauléon's Chevauchées
in Essex between December 1215 and January 1216*

Historical Note. Mountfitchet Castle

On page 40, Savary de Mauléon's taking and subsequent destruction of Mountfitchet Castle was described. However although the 'sieges' at Pleshey, Colchester and Castle Hedingham are documented, by contemporary chroniclers, there is no mention of Mountfitchet Castle. Of course Savary de Mauléon's assault on the castle would fit neatly into the time table of events during December 1215. However, an article by Katherine Fry about the Barons Montfichet found in the *Transactions of the Essex Archaeological Society, Vol. V*, dated 1873, suggests Mountfitchet Castle was slighted before Magna Carta was agreed. The Monfitchets were at odds with King John. Richard Monfitchet senior had been exiled, and in 1213 Montfichet's Tower in London was dismantled on royal orders. Fry admits her sources are unreliable but her conclusions are supported in general by other medieval experts. Needless to say the exile and then the destruction of the castle would have given Richard Montfitchet good cause to side with the rebel cause.

Part of the inside of the 20th century replica castle at Stansted Mountfitchet

Runnymede Hall in Thundersley opened in 1965

Colchester Castle. Changed hand five times but not as a result of a siege

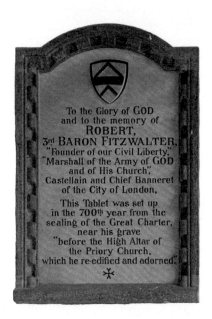

St Mary the Virgin, Little Dunmow

Robert de Vere
Hatfield Broad Oak

Grave stones of slain monks at Tilty

Harry Carter's road signs
on the B1383

King John Returns

King John left Berwick, Scotland, in late January 1216 and made his way south through Yorkshire, Nottinghamshire and Lincolnshire. He arrived at Bedford with his army during February. There he was joined by Savary de Mauléon and his men. In March they left Bedford together for Suffolk determined to bring those East Anglian castles which were still in rebel hands to heel. Framlingham Castle was the first objective. It was held by the Bigod family, major East Anglian landowners. Both Roger Bigod, 2nd Earl of Norfolk, and his son and heir Hugh were among the 25 council of barons opposing the king.

Framlingham castle was a strongly fortified castle. The king changed tactics. He sought to win control of the castle by a process of carrot and stick, rather than to destroy all before him. The carrot was that if the earl surrendered without a fight, swore allegiance to the king and above all paid a levy, he and his family would be spared. However the castle and all his lands would still be forfeit and in all probability the earl and his close family would be sent into exile. On the other hand, failure to surrender would bring the full might of the king to bear with little expectation of mercy.

Roger Bigod, on hearing word of the king's impending arrival, hastily departed to London with his personal retinue and as much of his treasure as they could carry. He left his constable, William Lenveise, in charge of the castle with just 50 men. Lenveise was placed in an unenviable catch 22 situation. He was not authorised to surrender the castle unless he was given permission to do so by his master, but Roger Bigod was absent and out of communication. Nevertheless, when the king's envoys arrived to negotiate, Lenveise weighed up the odds and agreed to surrender. The king promptly granted tenure of the castle to Savary de Mauléon. What happened to Lenveise is unknown.

After securing an easy victory at Framlingham, the combined royal forces returned emboldened to Colchester Castle, arriving on 14th March 1216. The king had sent envoys in advance to talk to the castle defenders but they had come back empty handed. William de Lanvallei, the castle's hereditary owner was absent. Yet the castle defenders, made up of English rebels and French troops loyal to Prince Louis, seemed in no mood to compromise.

Before a 'siege' took place it was the custom to *parley*. The *parley* (or negotiation) took place between the spokesmen of the besiegers and the defenders. They rode out on horseback and met about half way between the battle lines to discuss the terms of any surrender. If no agreement could be reached the siege began when the first shots were fired. Always fearing kidnap or ambush, King John and his advisors usually stayed well away from the *parley*, out of harm's way.

After five days outside Colchester the king withdrew to Ipswich. Two days later he came back to Colchester with reinforcements. The king offered the defenders free passage should they surrender. After some discussion the garrison agreed and on either the 23rd or 24th March the castle gates were opened. At this point John, true to form, reneged on part of the deal. Whilst the 115 French soldiers were allowed to travel freely to London, the Englishmen were shackled in chains and imprisoned. The castle had a new constable, Stephen Harengood was back.

The king's treachery considerably strained relationships between the English and their French allies. When the freed Frenchmen arrived in London they were greeted with extreme suspicion and there were even calls for them to be hanged as traitors. They were locked up, their eventual fate to be determined by Prince Louis when he arrived from France. The whole situation was aggravated further by the death of Pleshey's Geoffrey de Mandeville, who had been accidently killed in a tournament by Guillaume Acroce-Meure, a French knight.

King John's next move was to seize Castle Hedingham, less than a days' ride from Colchester and home of Robert de Vere, another rebel baron on the council of 25. Robert, the 3rd Earl of Oxford, had inherited the castle at Hedingham following the death of his elder brother Aubrey de Vere in October 1214. He had numerous grievances against King John. These included his having to pay substantial inheritance fees and the king's tardiness in confirming his earldom and appointment to the Office of Court Chamberlain, a hereditary right. According to Roger of Wendover, another medieval chronicler, Robert de Vere was one of the principal promoters of discontent.

Despite its sturdy outwards appearance, Castle Hedingham could not have withstood a determined siege. There was no moat and, with the main keep standing on dry land, the structure could easily be undermined. Royal forces arrived at Castle Hedingham on 25th March. For once the owner was in residence. Robert de Vere came out to parley with the king. By the 28th March, Hedingham Castle was the king's, together with the considerable de Vere estates. Robert de Vere had to swear allegiance to King John to escape with his life, although he had the satisfaction of knowing that his beloved castle was not being destroyed. Later that year however, de Vere transferred his allegiance to Prince Louis in London and carried on fighting. After the battle of Lincoln in 1217 he made his peace with the young Henry III and Castle Hedingham and all his lands were restored to him.

On 29th March 1217, John's forces moved to Pleshey Castle, presumably still in royal hands, then west across Essex to Canfield near Great Dunmow, Bishops Stortford and finally south to Waltham Abbey, arriving there on 31st March 1216.

This phase of the war came to an end. The king's winter and spring campaigns so far had seen the restoration of royal authority over most of the castles of the rebels in England and especially those of the east Anglian barons. The threat posed by the French Prince Louis had failed to materialise.

London, however, was still firmly in the grip of the rebels and two relatively small engagements soured the king's mood whilst giving a boost to the morale of his opponents. On 1st April, King John spent the night at Waltham Abbey.

According to Ralph of Coggeshall, the rebel Londoners, on hearing the king was nearby made ready for battle. It was a direct challenge. King John, as always reluctant to engage in open confrontation, sent out his trusted captain Savary de Mauléon to reconnoitre the Londoners' defences for possible weakness. It was a fateful move. The scouting party was ambushed and suffered heavy casualties and de Mauléon himself was seriously injured. Another group of King John's soldiers set forth to explore the possibility of attacking London from the river, or at least blockading the River Thames, but they too were set upon and 65 of their number killed, drowned or captured.

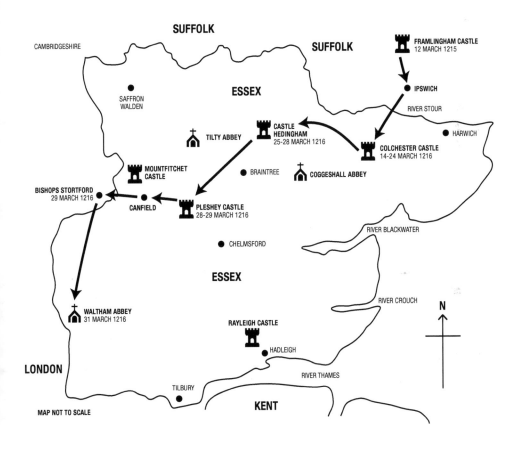

Kings John's route through Essex
March 1216

Death of the King

Although King John had suffered a few setbacks and was short of money, overall his campaign to subdue the rebellion was going well. The pope was still on his side and had excommunicated all those opposing him. Of course there was still the problem of rebel held London, but the city could not survive alone indefinitely. The king may have felt it was only a matter of time before surrender was offered.

After receiving intelligence that the threatened support for the rebels from Prince Louis was imminent, John headed for Kent to confront this claimant to his throne favoured by the rebel barons. All available English ships were summoned to Dover to intercept the enemy fleet when it appeared. The loyal garrison at Dover Castle, under the command of Hubert de Burgh, was reinforced and John ensured they were well supplied. He was confident that these measures would stop the French army landing. However in the event of the Frenchmen getting ashore, he had command of a sizeable army to repel them. Additionally, diplomatic efforts had been stepped up. Envoys sent to France had asked King Philip to stop his son (Louis) from continuing with his invasion plans. Unfortunately this all came to nothing. Philip left everybody guessing. He had many similar characteristics to John in that he was inclined to promise one thing and then do another.

English hopes were dashed completely when a huge storm blew up in the channel on 18th May, creating absolute chaos among the English ships at sea. The fleet was scattered and many vessels were so badly damaged they could only limp back into port for repairs. The English coast was left defenceless.

By 20th May 1216 the storm had abated. Prince Louis seized the opportunity and launched his invasion. According to Roger of Wendover, the French fleet was enormous, numbering upwards of 800 vessels. Louis, leading an advance flotilla of seven ships, made landfall on the Isle of Thanet on 21st May 1216. The full force of the French fleet arrived during the following day.

King John, from a vantage point at Sandwich, watched dumbstruck as hundreds of French sails filled the sea off the Kent coast and thousands of French fighting men poured ashore. Since 1066 English kings had regularly sent armies to France to wage war. Now the complete reverse had happened. According to another chronicler known as 'Anonymous of Bethune', the English army outnumbered the French by a factor of three to one. John could have fought the French on the beach or let them come ashore, attack them head on and drive them back into the sea. Instead he did neither. King John withdrew and fled west to Winchester.

Within ten days Prince Louis had secured Sandwich and Canterbury and retaken Rochester castle which had been subject to the long siege the previous November. At Rochester many of the rebel barons, including Robert Fitzwalter, Robert de Vere, William de Mandeville and Hugh Bigod came to pay homage to the man they hoped would be their new king. For Prince Louis it was a perfect start and on June 2nd he entered London to rapturous acclaim. Even the papal threats of excommunication meant little to the rebels. Most of the English churches simply ignored the edicts and twelve of the country's leading bishops welcomed Louis as the new defender of the English church.

For King John things went from bad to worse. Many of the barons who supported him changed sides and by August 1216 one third of England had submitted to Prince Louis. Nevertheless, success came with its share of difficulties. As one royalist castle after another yielded to Louis the victors began to argue over the spoils. The army fighting for Prince Louis consisted of baronial 'English' rebels, Frenchmen directly commanded by Louis and assorted mercenaries. The English became aggrieved when castles that fell were granted to French barons, who in many cases had never set foot in England before. Yet for the time being King John was still the common enemy binding the allies together. The seeds of division were there though and John was only too eager to exploit them when the opportunity arose. Louis had other problems too. Dover and Windsor castles, both strategic strong points from which counter attacks could be launched, remained stubbornly in the hands of forces loyal to King John. Both castles were under siege, which was costly in men and materials. To compound matters further, roving bands of archers, hiding out in the Weald of Kent, mounted hit and run attacks on the French supply lines.

During July and August 1216 Prince Louis pursued the king westwards but John was always one step ahead. The war settled into a stalemate. In September Louis' claim to the crown received a boost when the King of Scotland, Alexander II, after a perilous 400 mile journey south to Canterbury, paid homage to Louis "My great ally" referring to him as "King of the English".

While Alexander of Scotland was in Kent, King John left the West Country and headed to East Anglia on what turned out be his last campaign. Quite what his objective was is open to speculation. Some chroniclers have suggested his purpose was to capture the Scottish King as he returned to Scotland. Whatever the purpose, the campaign was wide ranging, energetic and noted for its brutality. The king was joined by Savary de Mauléon, who had recovered from his injuries in London, and together they set about the task with relish. During late September and early October the king's forces rampaged through Bedford, Cambridge, Peterborough, Lincoln and as far north as Boston and Grimsby. The king even managed a stop at Castle Hedingham on 18th September. The Benedictine monk and chronicler Matthew Paris described the activities of Savary de Mauléon as "burning his way through the countryside" and "perpetrating unheard of wickedness".

On 9th October King John was in King's Lynn, where according to Ralph of Coggeshall, "the king fell ill due to his insatiable gluttony". Two days later he left King's Lynn, heading west, and took a short cut at low tide across the five miles wide River Nene estuary, where it empties into the Wash. During the crossing the heavy baggage train became bogged down. Despite desperate efforts to pull the pack animals and carts free nearly all of the king's household goods, as well as the crown jewels, were lost as the rising tide engulfed them. Though historians through the ages have pondered the loss of the crown jewels there is no consensus as to exactly what happened or what was lost. Some, like Roger of Wendover, spoke of "the land opening up in the middle of the waves and causing whirlpools which sucked all in". What is agreed on is that John, already seriously ill, struggled on in great agony to arrive at Newark castle on the 18th October.

On the 19th October King John was dead.

The Battle for the English Crown

At Newark Castle King John knew he was near to death. He carefully arranged his affairs. He nominated his nine year old son Henry as his successor along with a Regency Council of barons that had stayed loyal to him to govern during Henry's minority. Letters were sent under the king's seal to all sheriffs and castellans in England ordering them to recognise Henry as the new sovereign and offering pardons and safe conduct to rebel barons who returned to the fold.

When King John's death became known, few mourned his passing. Many 'loyalists' had given their support, not out of duty but because they believed that through John their own vested interests were best served, old scores could be settled and they would receive a better share of the spoils. Chroniclers of the time were unanimous in condemning John as the man who despoiled his own people and England. Matthew Paris, writing some years later, typified their verdict when he wrote:-

With John's foul deeds all of England is stinking.

Even as John lay dead in Newark Castle he suffered a final indignity. His household staff helped themselves to as much as they could take of his remaining personal possessions, leaving not even enough cloth to afford his corpse a decent covering. Such was the fate of the king viewed by his subjects as an unstable despot.

On 28th October 1216, nine year old Henry III was crowned as the new English king. Two weeks later, on 12th November, the Regency Council elected their leader, the 70 year old William Marshal (also known as William the Marshall) to be the young king's protector. He quickly made a bold move to restore peace and order by reissuing a modified version of the Magna Carta. This time there was even backing from the new pope, Honorius III, who had come to office after the death of Innocent III in July 1216.

In just three weeks Prince Louis had lost his most important psychological assets. King John, whose villainy had united the English rebels behind Louis, was gone; a new untainted king had succeeded him to the throne and the Magna Carta that the barons had argued so vociferously for had been reissued with papal backing.

Yet in medieval society psychology and papal support was one thing. Brute force was another more important factor. The system of English government had all but broken down. Though Henry's forces under William Marshall were in control in the West Country and north of the Midlands, they could only pay their 'royalist', and mainly mercenary, forces by turning a blind eye to their widespread looting and terrorizing. Prince Louis and the rebels on the other hand, despite still holding London and most of Southern, Eastern and Central England, could not make any impression on the royalist strongholds of Dover, Windsor and Lincoln.

Louis' main problem was supply. Nearly everything; weapons, siege machines, extra manpower and finance had to be brought over from France. This was not only weather dependant but French ships were increasingly being harassed by English vessels operating in the channel. Hubert de Burgh's men, who held the strategically important Dover Castle, stubbornly resisted all rebel attempts to dislodge them. The siege was protracted and costly. In fact, with no end in sight, some of Prince Louis' supporters returned disheartened to France. More critically some English rebel barons, realising that Henry would be a different King to John and that he was English to boot, defected to King Henry.

Nevertheless, sufficient materials still arrived from France to enable Prince Louis to return to the offensive and early in 1217 he took a large part of his army west. Whilst the sieges of Dover, Windsor and Lincoln dragged on, his remaining force moved into Essex and East Anglia. By March, the castles at Pleshey, Hedingham, Colchester and Framlingham had fallen again into rebel hands.

Louis still needed more men and finance. In February he returned to France to drum up support for his cause. This left the rebellion in England without its main focus. Many of the French soldiers who had joined the Prince since the previous October were described as "the scum of the earth, riffraff and robbers". They did nothing to endear themselves to the resident population. For the local people the situation was awful in that both rebels and royalists took it in turn to rob and burn their houses and crops. No community could remain neutral. Any suspicion of support given to one side drew the ire of the other.

Prince Louis was absent for six weeks and when he returned to England he found a worsening military situation. There was no sign of a successful outcome to the sieges at Dover and Windsor. A number of lesser castles had fallen to the rebels but this success merely exacerbated tensions, particularly between French mercenaries and the English, as once again they argued over the spoils.

In late April 1217, Prince Louis gathered his forces to the west of London and decided to split them in two. One force, under the Comte de Perche, was sent north to Lincoln to secure both the castle and the town once and for all. The other, under the Prince himself, headed south. The journey north was marked by a storm of fire and savage looting all the way. Yet, the omens for a successful outcome in Lincoln for Louis were not good. He was haemorrhaging support from his English allies. Many thought a French king was not such a good idea and the new English one might not be so bad. Many allies suddenly made themselves unavailable or sat on the fence to see which way the wind blew. The churchmen, who swore loyalty to him the previous summer, withdrew their support and the brutal tactics of the prince's army in the field alienated almost everybody.

The Comte de Perche's force arrived in Lincoln and swiftly occupied most of the town. The castle, commanded by the formidable Nicola de la Haye, was a different matter though and despite the seemingly impossible odds she refused to surrender. The royalist side, newly invigorated under the leadership of William Marshal, was determined to ensure that such a strategically important stronghold should not be allowed to fall. A relief army mustered in nearby Newark then marched to Lincoln, avoiding the main road to confuse the enemy. The ruse worked and resulted in rebel spies miscounting the size of William's force. Consequently, the bulk of the rebel army stayed within the confines of Lincoln. The Marshal's army arrived in Lincoln on 20th May and the rebels found themselves trapped between it and the castle they were besieging.

In the ensuing skirmish the rebel leader, the Comte de Perche, was killed outside Lincoln Cathedral. Hemmed in, in the city's narrow streets, and realising the battle was lost, those rebels that were able to hastily fled; the rest surrendered. For Prince Louis the battle of Lincoln had been an unmitigated disaster. Nearly all the barons who had sworn loyalty to the prince had been captured, including Robert Fitzwalter, the leader of the council of 25, and Stansted's Richard de Montfitchet.

After the battle, the city was looted yet again, this time by the victors, on the pretext that the citizens had collaborated with the rebels. As a papal edict was in force excommunicating the entire clergy of Lincoln the cathedral was sacked too.

Prince Louis heard news of the defeat whilst directing the siege of Dover Castle. Survivors of the battle of Lincoln, who made it back to the relative safety of London, told graphic stories of being set upon by a uniformly hostile population in the countryside. Many fleeing foot soldiers were hacked to death by angry villagers on their journey south.

For Louis there was now a real fear that his main base in London would succumb to royalist overtures. Abandoning the siege of Dover he returned to the capital to bolster his power base while hoping that desperately needed supplies and reinforcements would arrive from France. In June 1217, a high level clerical delegation led by Guala Bicchieri, an Italian diplomat, arrived in London from Italy to try and negotiate a settlement but this came to nothing. There were more defections. William Marshal was quite confident that all he needed to do was wait. Meanwhile Prince Louis pinned his hopes on salvation from France.

The 24th August 1217 was noted as being a beautifully clear day. In Calais an expeditionary force of approximately 100 vessels laden with men, animals, weapons and siege machines set sail for England. By this time nationalistic lines were more distinct. The fleet heading for England from France was entirely French, whilst the ships coming out from England to intercept them were crewed by Englishmen. In the previous months William Marshal had come to realise more and more that the first line of defence for an island kingdom was the sea around its coast. The fledgling English 'Navy' had gradually been built up into a formidable fighting force. As soon as the French sails were sighted the English fleet, under the overall command of the master strategist of Dover, Hubert de Burgh, moved to intercept them.

The battle went England's way from the start. The heavily laden French ships, plodding their way across the channel, were an easy target. Their objective was to land much needed supplies in England. Instead the French fleet, maybe because of their much superior numbers, changed course and tried to pursue and engage the English vessels. They were no match for the more nimble English craft and one by one they were picked off in an exceptionally bloody sea battle. This resounding English success off the coast of Sandwich was even more significant than the victory achieved at Lincoln. Prince Louis had been dealt a crushing blow. His continental life line had been severed and vast amounts of valuable supplies had fallen into his enemies' hands.

In September, William Marshal could see that soon it would all be over. He ordered English ships to blockade the River Thames, making Louis effectively trapped in London. With most of the Prince's baronial supporters imprisoned in Lincoln and the possibility of breakout remote, the Marshal could tighten the noose around the capital as he chose.

Peace talks were held in Kingston and by 12th September terms were agreed. Prince Louis was to renounce his claim to the throne of England and annul the oaths of loyalty pledged by his baronial supporters. All prisoners on both sides were to be freed and their lands restored. Frenchmen in the service of Prince Louis were allowed to return to France unmolested. In their turn the rebel barons were obliged to swear allegiance to Henry III.

In order to hasten Louis' departure from England and remove any temptation on the part of King Philip of France to attempt to rescue his son, William Marshal offered Prince Louis an extremely generous financial settlement. On Wednesday 20th September Prince Louis met with his former enemies at Lambeth where both sides solemnly ratified the terms agreed at Kingston and enshrined them in the 'Treaty of Lambeth'. It marked the formal end to the war and the beginning of peace. The prince left London and was escorted to Dover by William Marshal and many leading barons. On 28th September Prince Louis set sail for France never to return.

The Barons

The Essex Rebels

Despite being on the losing side in the insurrection against King John and actively supporting Prince Louis in his bid take the English crown from nine year old Henry, the rebel barons came off remarkably unscathed. None of them were killed or injured 'in action' and although most were captured at the battle of Lincoln in May 1217, by all accounts being imprisoned there was not a particularly unhappy experience. Following the Treaty of Lambeth in September that year all the surviving barons regained their freedom and nearly all had their titles and lands restored.

Robert Fitzwalter, Lord of Dunmow, leader of the council of 25 and a man who had proclaimed himself *Marshal of the Army of God and the Holy Church,* was especially fortunate. In October 1217 he attended the great council held at Westminster where he and other former rebels swore allegiance to Henry III. Two years later, with the king's approval and the pope's blessing, he took part in the fifth crusade. After his return to England, Fitzwalter joined his old enemy Hubert de Burgh in helping the king to restore a number of wayward castellans (governors or constables of castles) to royal authority. Perhaps his final triumph was witnessing the confirmation of the Magna Carta and the Charter of the Forest in February 1225. Robert Fitzwalter died in December 1235, aged around 55, and was buried in Dunmow Priory. On his death Matthew Paris wrote a fulsome obituary saying that Fitzwalter,

> *Could match any earl in England and was valiant in arms, spirited and illustrious.*

Richard Montfitchet had the distinction of being the baron to live the longest after the sealing of the Magna Carta at Runnymede. He died, aged over seventy, in 1267. He was captured following the rebel defeat at Lincoln. After Prince Louis' departure from England, Richard Montfichet swore loyalty to King Henry and in return recovered his lands and rights, which included custody of his ancestral rights to Essex forest. Like Robert Fitzwalter he witnessed Henry III's reissue of the Magna Carta in 1225. He also served as sheriff of Essex and Hertfordshire.

Montfitchet was twice married but left no male heir. On his death his estates were divided among the children and grandchildren of his sisters.

William de Lanvallei III, the Lord of Walkern in Hertfordshire and the hereditary Constable of Colchester Castle, died shortly after the making of the Treaty of Lambeth. Lanvallei had the majority of his titles and lands, but not Colchester Castle, returned to him by the crown due to his 'return to obedience'. As part of the peace settlement, Colchester Castle acquired a new constable; the Bishop of London. During the barons' war, between 1215 and 1217, Colchester Castle changed hands five times. It was never captured as a result of an armed siege. All handovers were achieved by parleys (negotiations). William had family ties to Fitzwalter, whose niece was William's mother-in-law. He died, aged 25, in November 1217. The cause of death and where he was buried is not known. He left a wife and infant daughter named Hawise who became the ward of Hubert de Burgh and later married his son, John.

Robert de Vere, the 3rd Earl of Oxford, was the second surviving son of Aubrey, the 1st Earl, and his third wife, Agnes of Essex. He succeeded to the title on the death of his elder brother, another Aubrey, the 2nd Earl, in October 1214. Castle Hedingham had been the baronial seat of the de Vere family since the Norman Conquest. Robert stayed loyal to the cause of Prince Louis until the end. He then regained his castle and lands by swearing allegiance to Henry III in November 1217. He died in 1221 leaving a wife and young son, Hugh. He was buried in Hatfield Broad Oak Priory in Essex. One hundred years after his death an effigy in his honour was commissioned. This was later transferred to Hatfield Broad Oak parish church, a few miles south of present day Stansted airport.

Geoffrey de Mandeville, the 2nd Earl of Essex, inherited Pleshey Castle from his father Geoffrey FitzPeter, 1st Earl of Essex and long-serving Justiciar to King Richard I and King John. Geoffrey was the only rebel baron to meet an untimely end, in February 1216, and eighteen months before hostilities ceased. He was accidentally killed in a tournament by one of his allies, as opposed to in any hostile action from his enemies.

The One That Got Away

Geoffrey's younger brother, **William (Fitzgeoffrey) de Mandeville,** succeeded him to become the third Earl of Essex. Though not on the council of 25, William was active for the rebel cause and in May 1216 he travelled to Rochester to pay homage to Prince Louis. He was probably in London when Pleshey Castle was taken by Savary de Mauléon. A year later he fought under the Compte de Perche at the battle of Lincoln. Remarkably he was one of the few barons that managed to escape being trapped by William Marshall's forces and thus avoided capture. Nevertheless, after the Treaty of Lambeth, he too swore allegiance to Henry III. His estates were restored to him and in common with Robert Fitzwalter (the former baronial leader) he joined with his old enemies to help restore order in England. He later married Christine, the sister of his elder brother's first wife, and second daughter of Robert Fitzwalter. The **de Mandeville** family name ceased in 1227 when William died without an heir.

The Loyalist

Hubert de Burgh, the 1st Earl of Kent, rose from humble beginnings and was appointed Justiciar of England in King John's administration at the time of the sealing of the Magna Carta in June 1215. Chroniclers mention that de Burgh was one of the loyalists who advised the king to seal the charter. Despite some initial friction with William Marshal, de Burgh continued in this role under the youthful Henry III. Hubert de Burgh is remembered for his heroic defence of Dover castle from May 1216 to July 1217 and for his skill and later victory in commanding the English fleet during the battle of Sandwich which ended Prince Louis' claims to the English throne. Following the death of William Marshal, de Burgh became the dominant figure in the English government. He was extremely wealthy and had large land holdings in south Essex around Rayleigh and Hadleigh where King John originally had at least two hunting lodges. There is no surviving evidence of any warlike activity around Rayleigh castle during the insurrection. Around 1232, Henry III granted Hubert de Burgh a licence to build Hadleigh

Castle overlooking the Thames estuary, the prominent ruins of which survive today.

Shortly after the licence for Hadleigh castle was granted, Henry dismissed Hubert de Burgh and imprisoned him on the grounds of treason. Two years later he was pardoned but he never regained high ministerial office. He died in May 1243 in Surrey and was later buried at Blackfriars in London.

Geoffrey de Mandeville of Pleshey

Sculptures of Robert Fitzwalter, Robert de Vere, Geoffrey de Mandeville and Hubert de Burgh can be seen in the House of Lords. The House has eighteen statues of barons and high ranking clerical figures who helped secure the sealing of the Magna Carta. These were installed following a fire in Parliament in 1834. The statue of Geoffrey de Mandeville (of Pleshey) was lent to the British Library for the 2015 *Magna Carta: Law, Liberty, Legacy* exhibition.

In fact it could be said that Geoffrey de Mandeville of Pleshey featured as the 'face' of the exhibition.

A Small World

The Magna Carta barons were interconnected through family ties and marriage - no matter whether they were the best of friends or bitterest of enemies. The leader of the baronial council of twenty five was Robert Fitzwalter. His daughter Matilda was the wife of Geoffrey de Mandeville (of Pleshey). According to many of the chroniclers Matilda was, to put it politely, subject to the roving eye of King John, which naturally caused friction with the king on the part of both Fitzwalter and Mandeville. On Matilda's death, however, Geoffrey married the divorced wife of King John, Isabella Countess of Gloucester, who, after Geoffrey's death, married Hubert de Burgh!

As we have seen in the last chapter, another family connection was between Hawise, the daughter of Colchester's William de Lanvallei III, and Hubert de Burgh's son John. Their granddaughter subsequently married Robert, the grandson of Robert Fitzwalter. Raymond de Burgh, Hubert's nephew's son, was the second husband of Christine Fitzwalter, the widow of William de Mandeville and daughter of Robert Fitzwalter.

For the de Veres, Robert de Vere married Isobel de Bolebec, the daughter of Richard de Montfitchet's sister Margaret. His brother Aubrey's second marriage was to Alice Bigod, the daughter of Roger Bigod of nearby Framlingham Castle in Suffolk. Robert's aunt, Juliana de Vere, was the first wife of Hugh Bigod. Their son Roger Bigod, the 2nd Earl of Norfolk, married Ida, Countess of Norfolk, and their son, another Hugh and the 3rd Earl, married Matilda, a daughter of William Marshal, the arch opponent of the rebel cause.

William de Forz, 3rd Earl of Albemarle, the son of William de Mandeville and Hawise, Countess of Aumale, was another rebel baron, although he changed sides a few times when it suited him. He was allowed to inherit his mother's English lands on the condition that he married Aveline, another sister of Richard de Montfitchet. Their son William, the 4th Earl, grew up with a Montfitchet uncle and mother and de Veres as cousins.

The above are just a few examples of baronial family make up in the 13th century in England - it was indeed a small world.

The Charter of the Forest
(The Magna Carta comes of age)

'The Articles of the Barons' was the document sealed by King John in June 1215 and then reissued in 1216, with changes to appease the rebels, as the Great Charter, in the name of Henry III. It was not yet known as the Magna Carta. Two years after the great ceremony at Runnymede, on November 6th 1217, a new document was issued, the *Charter of the Forest*. (Original copies of this charter can be seen in the British Library and in Lincoln Castle; sadly they are unreadable since they are written in medieval Latin). There were now two charters in operation, the original and this latest one, drafted to deal exclusively with a range of hugely contentious issues relating to forest matters. Three months later, in February 1218, the term 'Magna Carta' first appeared in a royal proclamation. The name had been chosen to avoid confusion between the Great Charter and the smaller 'Forest Charter'.

In contrast to the Magna Carta, which dealt mainly with the rights of barons, the Charter of the Forest offered some rights and protections to the 'common people' from the abuses inflicted on them by their feudal overlords or royal officials. It has to be remembered that the royal forests contained huge swathes of land suitable for grazing as well as being a vitally important source of fuel for cooking and heating.

The Forest Charter resulted in numerous tracts of Essex forest lands being returned to their ancestral owners and a process of disafforestation throughout the county was begun. Lands that had been arbitrarily classified as 'forest' by both King John and King Richard, and therefore subject to 'Forest Law', i.e., the King's whim, were immediately returned to their former status. Within a relatively short space of time most of the north of the county was no longer subject to the vagaries of 'Forest Law' and some of its more draconian practises. For example, Clause 10 of the Charter of the Forest decreed that, "No man shall henceforth lose life or limb because of our venison (i.e. poaching the king's game)". Instead offenders would be heavily fined or "if without means, shall lie in our prison for a year and a day".

The new charter also streamlined the forest court system. Perhaps the most important change was that the sovereign was no longer the sole arbiter of all matters relating to the forest. People who lived in areas neighbouring the forest were no longer obliged to attend forest courts unless they had been specifically charged with a forest offence. Impositions of collective punishment, where one of member of a community failed to pay a fine, were largely discontinued. Penalties pertaining to the clawing of dogs no longer allowed for the offenders' oxen to be seized as redress. The powers of the mercenary 'Foresters in Fee' were curtailed and witness of an offence, or testimony, was required from 'law-worthy men and not otherwise'. *Chiminage*, the arbitrary exacting of tolls on travellers passing through the forest by self-appointed toll collectors, was outlawed. There was also a general amnesty for many offenders who had been waiting years for their cases to be heard in a forest court.

In general the new charter re-established the rights of access to the forest that had been eroded by a succession of kings and afforded a degree of economic protection for everybody who used the forest to forage for food or fuel and to graze their animals.

Yet, despite two years of warfare and fine new charters being issued, it is debatable how much the lot of the 'common man' improved. Most were still tied to their feudal overlord with no realistic means of escape. During the war it was the 'common man' who was likely to find his village and home burnt, and his crops and livestock stolen, by marauding armies of either side. Those men who were pressed into military service on behalf of their master were more than likely to be the first to be sacrificed if the battle went badly and, if captured they were frequently left to starve in their opponent's jails or used as forced labour as they had no ransom value.

Whilst the Charter of the Forest imposed some curbs on royalty within the forest, it gave the barons an unprecedented degree of freedom to do as they wished with the forest under their control. Over time the fate of the forest would prove to be determined not by the pleasures of a privileged few but by hard commercial interests.

The forest was no longer a rich man's playground or a means of survival for the poor. It was a resource to be exploited and from which to make money.

The Demise of Essex Forest

Copies of the original Charter of the Forest can be seen in the British Library or alternatively at Lincoln Castle. Over the passage of time many of the clauses in the charter have fallen into disuse but those still relevant were incorporated into 20th century English law. At the time of the Magna Carta all of Essex was deemed to be forest. Today the once great forest of Essex has all but disappeared. From 1215 onwards the forest was gradually squeezed and pushed into the south and the south western corner of the county. Epping Forest is the nucleus which remains.

In the early 13th century, although the forest was still a hunting preserve for royalty, it was the major source of timber for castle building or repair, housing and the building of ships. Even King John recognised the strategic need for timber. The following entry is from the king's official correspondence in 1214.

> "To the Sheriff of Essex. We order you to find ships to carry the timber, which has been felled in the park of Ralegh (Rayleigh) and taken to the water, to Dover for work in Dover Castle".

Some three centuries later, in the Tudor era, the forest areas were under siege as thousands of trees were felled to supply the navy and the rapidly expanding merchant fleet. Yet the largely defunct forest law still had its uses, one of which was to boost royal coffers by relieving the burgeoning new rich (and ignorant?) of some of their wealth. In 1563, the well to do Roger Appleton of Benfleet, heading a family consortium, paid the young Queen Elizabeth I the substantial sum of £500 to have an area around Rayleigh 'released' from forest law. It may have been a case of sharp practice on the part of royal officials or perhaps, more intriguingly, an old fool having his head turned by a young woman. In any event the area in question had been released from most of the strictures of forest law for hundreds of years.

One hundred years later, under Oliver Cromwell, the Lord Protector, the demise of the forest accelerated. Cromwell regarded royal hunting for the privileged with disdain and, equally, had no particular feeling for the 'commoners' ancient rights. He viewed the forest as an asset to be harvested but seemed happy to allow his supporters to enclose areas of the forest for their own use.

It is doubtful whether any forest would have survived at all as a public open space during the Victorian era, if it hadn't been for the efforts of a hardy few. In 1849, Hainault Forest (part of the Great Forest of Waltham) was a huge area in south west Essex occupying over 17,000 acres. It was a prime source of timber for the navy. Oak taken from Hainault was used to build the *Victory* and the *Temeraire*.

Despite the age of sail coming to an end and wooden ships being replaced by iron, steam driven ships, the Government was under huge commercial pressure from developers and landowners to enclose the forest and keep the public out. After several attempts and much parliamentary chicanery the 'Disafforestation of Hainault Forest Act' was passed in the summer of 1851.

The ink was hardly dry on the royal assent before the destruction of the forest began in earnest. Within six weeks, 100,000 trees were felled and 3,000 acres of woodland cleared using specially built steam powered machines that could uproot a whole tree in minutes. The destruction caused public uproar and, after much of the felled timber was simply left to rot, one critic described it as "state sponsored vandalism on an unprecedented scale". What remains of the forest today lies within the Hainault Forest Country Park, south of Chigwell Row and bordered by Romford Road to the west. It is one fiftieth of the size it was in 1850.

The next target of the developers was Epping Forest. As London expanded, vast swathes of the forest were fenced off and enclosed. Trees were cut down to make way for housing, industry, railways or agriculture. The forest was also supposedly infested by criminals and thieves. The likes of Dick Turpin and his gang had hidden in the forest some years before.

In 1858 the crown (acting in the name of Queen Victoria) exercised its somewhat dubious forest rights again and sold off 1,400 acres of Epping Forest to William Whitaker Maitland, the then Lord of the Manor at Loughton. However, dating from the time of the Magna Carta and confirmed again in a charter by Queen Elizabeth I, certain ancient rights granted to householders who lived in and around the forest were still in force. They could still cut wood for fuel and graze their cattle within the forest. Strict rules were laid down for the practice of cutting wood, known as lopping. Lopping was permitted on Mondays only, between 11th November and St. George's Day, 23rd April. Wood acquired had to be removed on sledges, not wheeled carts, and had to be burnt as domestic fuel and not be sold or used for any trade purpose. The grandson of William Whitaker Maitland, the Reverend John Maitland, decided he would sell most of his manor for housing and in the process ban lopping from the estate.

Thomas Willingale, a 'commoner' of Loughton, had other ideas. He jealously maintained his rights to lop. Despite the best efforts of Maitland to trick him into forfeiting his lopping rights, Willingale managed to outwit him at every turn. Thomas soon acquired a nickname – the Lopper of Loughton.

Maitland's next move (with the clandestine backing of the local board of works) was to prosecute Willingale and his fellow loppers and for 10 years a legal game of cat and mouse took place. Thomas died in 1870 but his son, Sam, took up the standard of the loppers. Over the years several fines were imposed on the Willingales. Most of these were not paid and Sam even spent some time in prison for non-payment. The case became a cause célèbre and was viewed as a David and Goliath contest. Sam attracted considerable moral, and then financial, support from the City of London and the House of Commons. There was still lingering outrage at the way much of Hainault Forest had been destroyed 20 years earlier. Now alarm bells were ringing at the way huge areas of Epping Forest were being fenced off for the personal gain of a few rich land owners, whilst the public were denied access. The tables were then turned and Maitland was confronted by a series of legal challenges, undertaken by the Corporation of London, which culminated in the passing of the Epping Forest Act of 1878. Amongst other things, the act declared that all the enclosures made by land owners in the previous 25 years were illegal. Henceforth, the forest was to become a public open space. The forest had been saved and unwittingly the Lopper of Loughton, Thomas Willingale, had been its guiding saviour.

Four years later, in May 1882, Queen Victoria was on the side of the people. At a ceremony at High Beech she addressed an audience of 2,000 and declared, "It gives me the greatest satisfaction to dedicate this beautiful forest to the use and enjoyment of my people for all time". From that time Epping became "The people's forest and the forest for all".

What remains of Epping Forest, lying in the north and east of the London Borough of Waltham Forest, has shrunk considerably from its former size. It stretches from Forest Gate in the south for approximately twelve miles north to Epping. Its widest point is five miles. Although mostly wooded it also has areas of grassland, heath, rivers and ponds. It is managed today by the Corporation of London.

Epping Forest. The Peoples Forest. Open to all.

The 'Last' Forest

Hatfield Forest is an anomaly. It lies immediately south of Stansted airport and just to the east of the M11 in the parish of Hatfield Broad Oak, occupying just over 1,000 acres. It has been described by Oliver Rackman, the botanist and expert on the countryside, as "a rare surviving example of a medieval hunting forest that is unique in England. Hatfield is a place where one can step back to the Middle Ages to see, with only a little imagination, what a forest looked like". It is not a forest of thickly wooded trees but an open landscape dotted with areas of woodland which enabled the royal huntsman to ride at full gallop in pursuit of their quarry. It is also one of the largest areas in East Anglia that has never been ploughed.

Designated a Royal Hunting Forest by Henry I, it was sold in 1238 by Henry III, who maintained his hunting rights. Hatfield forest then had a succession of owners who included Robert the Bruce, Henry Stafford the Duke of Buckingham (executed by Henry VII) and the notorious Sir Richard

Hatfield Broad Oak Church in the early 1800s

Riche, once ranked in a BBC poll as the third worst Briton of the last 1,000 years. In 1729 the forest was acquired by the Houblon family, who retained ownership until 1923, when the great conservationist and Liberal Party politician, Edward North Buxton purchased it and immediately donated it to the National Trust.

Hatfield Forest is the last 'original' forest and considering the number of owners it has had through the ages it is truly remarkable it has survived virtually untouched into the 20th century.

Unusual (Essex) Connections

There are numerous Essex connections to Magna Carta. Many we have covered, such as the individual Essex barons on the council of 25 who were charged with enforcing the charter. There are the Essex castles that were laid siege to during the Barons' War, the abbeys that were raided by mercenary forces and the Essex churches that were also attacked and still contain physical legacies of incidents related to the Magna Carta. We have mentioned the great chronicler of the day, Ralph of Coggeshall, and noted King John's hunting lodges at Writtle and Thundersley and Richard de Monfitchet's ownership of the land at Runnymede.

In 1215 most of Essex was designated forest. The county naturally was subject to the vagaries of 'Forest Law' and the Charter of the Forest and the subsequent demise of the forests greatly affected Essex. In the last chapter we considered the anomaly of Hatfield Forest and how it mysteriously survived more or less untouched over the centuries.

Yet there are some odd connections not obviously apparent and, despite a great deal of research, there is no satisfactory answer as to why these connections exist. Around the county there are thoroughfares named after Fitzwalter such as Fitzwalter Road in Colchester or Fitzwalter Lane in Danbury and in Langdon Hills there is a Mandeville Way.

In 1211 'King John's Hunting Lodge' was built in the north of Writtle. It comprised a series of low buildings, which even included a jail, all enclosed by a moat. 'Hunting Lodge' was a term frequently used to describe early medieval royal residences. Sometimes the lodge was known as 'The King's House' or 'King John's Palace'. During the reign of John's son, Henry III, the Writtle Lodge was sold. The buildings remained until the mid-1950's when the remains were demolished to make way for Writtle Agricultural College. The medieval fish ponds which had survived were converted into a reservoir.

Further south in the county, in Benfleet, there was a hunting lodge in The Chase, Thundersley and another at Jarvis Hall in Thundersley Park Road. During 1214, King John is reputed to have stayed at this 'palace' near Kenneth Road and was quite possibly entertained by Hubert de Burg, the builder of nearby Hadleigh Castle. King John's School in

Shipwrights Drive is alleged to have been built on the site of a royal hunting lodge.

For some reason Benfleet seems to have taken King John and its Magna Carta connections to heart. The King John School was opened on 2nd May 1949 and it is the only school in Essex so named.

THE KING JOHN SCHOOL

The Chase in Thundersley, mentioned above, was renamed Runnymede Chase sometime between 1945 and 1953. Behind the Castle Point Borough Council Offices in Kiln Road, lies Runnymede Hall and Runnymede Swimming Pool. Runnymede Hall was officially opened by Councillor Ron Williams on the 10th December 1965, the year being the 750th anniversary

RUNNYMEDE CHASE
RUNNYMEDE ROAD

of the sealing of the Magna Carta.

More curious is Runnymede Road on Canvey Island which was adopted in the late 1960s. There is another Runnymede Road, adopted in the 1950s, in Stanford-le-Hope by the train station.

What is perhaps strangest of all, considering the significance of the name Runnymede to the national psyche, is that all roads, streets or public buildings carrying the name Runnymede in Essex are to be found (apart from one in nearby Stanford-le-Hope) in the County Borough of Castle Point.

The Magna Carta Text in Full (1215)

JOHN, by the grace of God King of England, Lord of Ireland, Duke of Normandy and Aquitaine, and Count of Anjou, to his archbishops, bishops, abbots, earls, barons, justices, foresters, sheriffs, stewards, servants, and to all his officials and loyal subjects, Greeting. KNOW THAT BEFORE GOD, for the health of our soul and those of our ancestors and heirs, to the honour of God, the exaltation of the holy Church, and the better ordering of our kingdom, at the advice of our reverend fathers Stephen, archbishop of Canterbury, primate of all England, and cardinal of the holy Roman Church, Henry archbishop of Dublin, William bishop of London, Peter bishop of Winchester, Jocelin bishop of Bath and Glastonbury, Hugh bishop of Lincoln, Walter bishop of Worcester, William bishop of Coventry, Benedict bishop of Rochester, Master Pandulf subdeacon and member of the papal household, Brother Aymeric master of the knighthood of the Temple in England, William Marshal earl of Pembroke, William earl of Salisbury, William earl of Warren, William earl of Arundel, Alan of Galloway constable of Scotland, Warin fitz Gerald, Peter fitz Herbert, Hubert de Burgh seneschal of Poitou, Hugh de Neville, Matthew fitz Herbert, Thomas Basset, Alan Basset, Philip Daubeny, Robert de Roppeley, John Marshal, John fitz Hugh, and other loyal subjects.

1. FIRST, THAT WE HAVE GRANTED TO GOD, and by this present charter have confirmed for us and our heirs in perpetuity, that the English Church shall be free, and shall have its rights undiminished, and its liberties unimpaired. That we wish this so to be observed, appears from the fact that of our own free will, before the outbreak of the present dispute between us and our barons, we granted and confirmed by charter the freedom of the Church's elections - a right reckoned to be of the greatest necessity and importance to it - and caused this to be confirmed by Pope Innocent III. This freedom we shall observe ourselves, and desire to be observed in good faith by our heirs in perpetuity. TO ALL FREE MEN OF OUR KINGDOM we have also granted, for us and our heirs for ever, all the liberties written out below, to have and to keep for them and their heirs, of us and our heirs.

2. If any earl, baron, or other person that holds lands directly of the Crown, for military service, shall die, and at his death his heir shall be of full age and owe a 'relief', the heir shall have his inheritance on payment of the ancient scale of 'relief'. That is to say, the heir or heirs of an earl shall pay £100 for the entire earl's barony, the heir or heirs of a knight 100s. at most for the entire knight's 'fee', and any man that owes less shall pay less, in accordance with the ancient usage of 'fees'.

3. But if the heir of such a person is under age and a ward, when he comes of age he shall have his inheritance without 'relief' or fine.

4. The guardian of the land of an heir who is under age shall take from it only reasonable revenues, customary dues, and feudal services. He shall do this without destruction or damage to men or property. If we have given the guardianship of the land to a sheriff, or to any person answerable to us for the revenues, and he commits destruction or damage, we will exact compensation from him, and the land shall be entrusted to two worthy and prudent men of the same 'fee', who shall be answerable to us for the revenues, or to the person to whom we have assigned them. If we have given or sold to anyone the guardianship of such land, and he causes destruction or damage, he shall lose the guardianship of it, and it shall be handed over to two worthy and prudent men of the same 'fee', who shall be similarly answerable to us.

5. For so long as a guardian has guardianship of such land, he shall maintain the houses, parks, fish preserves, ponds, mills, and everything else pertaining to it, from the revenues of the land itself. When the heir comes of age, he shall restore the whole land to him, stocked with plough teams and such implements of husbandry as the season demands and the revenues from the land can reasonably bear.

6. Heirs may be given in marriage, but not to someone of lower social standing. Before a marriage takes place, it shall be made known to the heir's next-of-kin.

7. At her husband's death, a widow may have her marriage portion and inheritance at once and without trouble. She shall pay nothing for her dower, marriage portion, or any inheritance that she and her husband held jointly on the day of his death. She may remain in her husband's house for forty days after his death, and within this period her dower shall be assigned to her.

8. No widow shall be compelled to marry, so long as she wishes to remain without a husband. But she must give security that she will not marry without royal consent, if she holds her lands of the Crown, or without the consent of whatever other lord she may hold them of.

9. Neither we nor our officials will seize any land or rent in payment of a debt, so long as the debtor has movable goods sufficient to discharge the debt. A debtor's sureties shall not be distrained upon so long as the debtor himself can discharge his debt. If, for lack of means, the debtor is unable to discharge his debt, his sureties shall be answerable for it. If they so desire, they may have the debtor's lands and rents until they have received satisfaction for the debt that they paid for him, unless the debtor can show that he has settled his obligations to them. *

10. If anyone who has borrowed a sum of money from Jews dies before the debt has been repaid, his heir shall pay no interest on the debt for so long as he remains under age, irrespective of whom he holds his lands. If such a debt falls into the hands of the Crown, it will take nothing except the principal sum specified in the bond. *

11. If a man dies owing money to Jews, his wife may have her dower and pay nothing towards the debt from it. If he leaves children that are under age, their needs may also be provided for on a scale appropriate to the size of his holding of lands. The debt is to be paid out of the residue, reserving the service due to his feudal lords. Debts owed to persons other than Jews are to be dealt with similarly. *

12. No 'scutage' or 'aid' may be levied in our kingdom without its general consent, unless it is for the ransom of our person, to make our eldest son a knight, and (once) to marry our eldest daughter. For these purposes only a reasonable 'aid' may be levied. 'Aids' from the city of London are to be treated similarly.

13. The city of London shall enjoy all its ancient liberties and free customs, both by land and by water. We also will and grant that all other cities, boroughs, towns, and ports shall enjoy all their liberties and free customs. *

14. To obtain the general consent of the realm for the assessment of an 'aid' - except in the three cases specified above - or a 'scutage', we will cause the archbishops, bishops, abbots, earls, and greater barons to be summoned individually by letter. To those who hold lands directly of us we will cause a general summons to be issued, through the sheriffs and other officials, to come together on a fixed day (of which at least forty days notice shall be given) and at a fixed place. In all letters of summons, the cause of the summons will be stated. When a summons has been issued, the business appointed for the day shall go forward in accordance with the resolution of those present, even if not all those who were summoned have appeared.*

15. In future we will allow no one to levy an 'aid' from his free men, except to ransom his person, to make his eldest son a knight, and (once) to marry his eldest daughter. For these purposes only a reasonable 'aid' may be levied.

16. No man shall be forced to perform more service for a knight's 'fee', or other free holding of land, than is due from it.

17. Ordinary lawsuits shall not follow the royal court around, but shall be held in a fixed place.

18. Inquests of novel disseisin, mort d'ancestor, and darrein presentment shall be taken only in their proper county court. We ourselves, or in our absence

abroad our chief justice, will send two justices to each county four times a year, and these justices, with four knights of the county elected by the county itself, shall hold the assizes in the county court, on the day and in the place where the court meets.

19. If any assizes cannot be taken on the day of the county court, as many knights and freeholders shall afterwards remain behind, of those who have attended the court, as will suffice for the administration of justice, having regard to the volume of business to be done.

20. For a trivial offence, a free man shall be fined only in proportion to the degree of his offence, and for a serious offence correspondingly, but not so heavily as to deprive him of his livelihood. In the same way, a merchant shall be spared his merchandise, and a villein the implements of his husbandry, if they fall upon the mercy of a royal court. None of these fines shall be imposed except by the assessment on oath of reputable men of the neighbourhood.

21. Earls and barons shall be fined only by their equals, and in proportion to the gravity of their offence.

22. A fine imposed upon the lay property of a clerk in holy orders shall be assessed upon the same principles, without reference to the value of his ecclesiastical benefice.

23. No town or person shall be forced to build bridges over rivers except those with an ancient obligation to do so.

24. No sheriff, constable, coroners, or other royal officials are to hold lawsuits that should be held by the royal justices. *

25. Every county, hundred, wapentake, and tithing shall remain at its ancient rent, without increase, except the royal demesne manors.

26. If at the death of a man who holds a lay 'fee' of the Crown, a sheriff or royal official produces royal letters patent of summons for a debt due to the Crown, it shall be lawful for them to seize and list movable goods found in the lay 'fee' of the dead man to the value of the debt, as assessed by worthy men. Nothing shall be removed until the whole debt is paid, when the residue shall be given over to the executors to carry out the dead man's will. If no debt is due to the Crown, all the movable goods shall be regarded as the property of the dead man, except the reasonable shares of his wife and children. *

27. If a free man dies intestate, his movable goods are to be distributed by his next-of-kin and friends, under the supervision of the Church. The rights of his debtors are to be preserved.

28. No constable or other royal official shall take corn or other movable goods from any man without immediate payment, unless the seller voluntarily offers postponement of this.

29. No constable may compel a knight to pay money for castle-guard if the knight is willing to undertake the guard in person, or with reasonable excuse to supply some other fit man to do it. A knight taken or sent on military service shall be excused from castle-guard for the period of this service.

30. No sheriff, royal official, or other person shall take horses or carts for transport from any free man, without his consent.

31. Neither we nor any royal official will take wood for our castle, or for any other purpose, without the consent of the owner.

32. We will not keep the lands of people convicted of felony in our hand for longer than a year and a day, after which they shall be returned to the lords of the 'fees' concerned.

33. All fish-weirs shall be removed from the Thames, the Medway, and throughout the whole of England, except on the sea coast.

34. The writ called precipe shall not in future be issued to anyone in respect of any holding of land, if a free man could thereby be deprived of the right of trial in his own lord's court.

35. There shall be standard measures of wine, ale, and corn (the London quarter), throughout the kingdom. There shall also be a standard width of dyed cloth, russet, and haberject, namely two ells within the selvedges. Weights are to be standardised similarly.

36. In future nothing shall be paid or accepted for the issue of a writ of inquisition of life or limbs. It shall be given gratis, and not refused.

37. If a man holds land of the Crown by 'fee-farm', 'socage', or 'burgage', and also holds land of someone else for knight's service, we will not have guardianship of his heir, nor of the land that belongs to the other person's 'fee', by virtue of the 'fee-farm', 'socage', or 'burgage', unless the 'fee-farm' owes knight's service. We will not have the guardianship of a man's heir, or of land that he holds of someone else, by reason of any small property that he may hold of the Crown for a service of knives, arrows, or the like.

38. In future no official shall place a man on trial upon his own unsupported statement, without producing credible witnesses to the truth of it.

39. No free man shall be seized or imprisoned, or stripped of his rights or possessions, or outlawed or exiled, or deprived of his standing in any way, nor will we proceed with force against him, or send others to do so, except by the lawful judgment of his equals or by the law of the land.

40. To no one will we sell, to no one deny or delay right or justice.

41. All merchants may enter or leave England unharmed and without fear, and may stay or travel within it, by land or water, for purposes of trade, free from all illegal exactions, in accordance with ancient and lawful customs. This,

however, does not apply in time of war to merchants from a country that is at war with us. Any such merchants found in our country at the outbreak of war shall be detained without injury to their persons or property, until we or our chief justice have discovered how our own merchants are being treated in the country at war with us. If our own merchants are safe they shall be safe too. *

42. In future it shall be lawful for any man to leave and return to our kingdom unharmed and without fear, by land or water, preserving his allegiance to us, except in time of war, for some short period, for the common benefit of the realm. People that have been imprisoned or outlawed in accordance with the law of the land, people from a country that is at war with us, and merchants - who shall be dealt with as stated above - are excepted from this provision.

43. If a man holds lands of any 'escheat' such as the 'honour' of Wallingford, Nottingham, Boulogne, Lancaster, or of other 'escheats' in our hand that are baronies, at his death his heir shall give us only the 'relief' and service that he would have made to the baron, had the barony been in the baron's hand. We will hold the 'escheat' in the same manner as the baron held it.

44. People who live outside the forest need not in future appear before the royal justices of the forest in answer to general summonses, unless they are actually involved in proceedings or are sureties for someone who has been seized for a forest offence. *

45. We will appoint as justices, constables, sheriffs, or other officials, only men that know the law of the realm and are minded to keep it well.

46. All barons who have founded abbeys, and have charters of English kings or ancient tenure as evidence of this, may have guardianship of them when there is no abbot, as is their due.

47. All forests that have been created in our reign shall at once be disafforested. River-banks that have been enclosed in our reign shall be treated similarly. *

48. All evil customs relating to forests and warrens, foresters, warreners, sheriffs and their servants, or river-banks and their wardens, are at once to be investigated in every county by twelve sworn knights of the county, and within forty days of their enquiry the evil customs are to be abolished completely and irrevocably. But we, or our chief justice if we are not in England, are first to be informed. *

49. We will at once return all hostages and charters delivered up to us by Englishmen as security for peace or for loyal service. *

50. We will remove completely from their offices the kinsmen of Gerard de Athée, and in future they shall hold no offices in England. The people in question are Engelard de Cigogné, Peter, Guy, and Andrew de Chanceaux, Guy

de Cigogné, Geoffrey de Martigny and his brothers, Philip Marc and his brothers, with Geoffrey his nephew, and all their followers. *

51. As soon as peace is restored, we will remove from the kingdom all the foreign knights, bowmen, their attendants, and the mercenaries that have come to it, to its harm, with horses and arms. *

52. To any man whom we have deprived or dispossessed of lands, castles, liberties, or rights, without the lawful judgment of his equals, we will at once restore these. In cases of dispute the matter shall be resolved by the judgment of the twenty-five barons referred to below in the clause for securing the peace (see 61). In cases, however, where a man was deprived or dispossessed of something without the lawful judgment of his equals by our father King Henry or our brother King Richard, and it remains in our hands or is held by others under our warranty, we shall have respite for the period commonly allowed to Crusaders, unless a lawsuit had been begun, or an enquiry had been made at our order, before we took the Cross as a Crusader. On our return from the Crusade, or if we abandon it, we will at once render justice in full. *

53. We shall have similar respite in rendering justice in connexion with forests that are to be disafforested, or to remain forests, when these were first afforested by our father Henry or our brother Richard; with the guardianship of lands in another person's 'fee', when we have hitherto had this by virtue of a 'fee' held of us for knight's service by a third party; and with abbeys founded in another person's 'fee', in which the lord of the 'fee' claims to own a right. On our return from the Crusade, or if we abandon it, we will at once do full justice to complaints about these matters.

54. No one shall be arrested or imprisoned on the appeal of a woman for the death of any person except her husband. *

55. All fines that have been given to us unjustly and against the law of the land, and all fines that we have exacted unjustly, shall be entirely remitted or the matter decided by a majority judgment of the twenty-five barons referred to below in the clause for securing the peace (see 61) together with Stephen, archbishop of Canterbury, if he can be present, and such others as he wishes to bring with him. If the archbishop cannot be present, proceedings shall continue without him, provided that if any of the twenty-five barons has been involved in a similar suit himself, his judgment shall be set aside, and someone else chosen and sworn in his place, as a substitute for the single occasion, by the rest of the twenty-five.

56. If we have deprived or dispossessed any Welshmen of land, liberties, or anything else in England or in Wales, without the lawful judgment of their equals, these are at once to be returned to them. A dispute on this point shall be

determined in the Marches by the judgment of equals. English law shall apply to holdings of land in England, Welsh law to those in Wales, and the law of the Marches to those in the Marches. The Welsh shall treat us and ours in the same way. *

57. In cases where a Welshman was deprived or dispossessed of anything, without the lawful judgment of his equals, by our father King Henry or our brother King Richard, and it remains in our hands or is held by others under our warranty, we shall have respite for the period commonly allowed to Crusaders, unless a lawsuit had been begun, or an enquiry had been made at our order, before we took the Cross as a Crusader. But on our return from the Crusade, or if we abandon it, we will at once do full justice according to the laws of Wales and the said regions. *

58. We will at once return the son of Llywelyn, all Welsh hostages, and the charters delivered to us as security for the peace. *

59. With regard to the return of the sisters and hostages of Alexander, king of Scotland, his liberties and his rights, we will treat him in the same way as our other barons of England, unless it appears from the charters that we hold from his father William, formerly king of Scotland, that he should be treated otherwise. This matter shall be resolved by the judgment of his equals in our court.

60. All these customs and liberties that we have granted shall be observed in our kingdom in so far as concerns our own relations with our subjects. Let all men of our kingdom, whether clergy or laymen, observe them similarly in their relations with their own men. *

61. SINCE WE HAVE GRANTED ALL THESE THINGS for God, for the better ordering of our kingdom, and to allay the discord that has arisen between us and our barons, and since we desire that they shall be enjoyed in their entirety, with lasting strength, for ever, we give and grant to the barons the following security: The barons shall elect twenty-five of their number to keep, and cause to be observed with all their might, the peace and liberties granted and confirmed to them by this charter. If we, our chief justice, our officials, or any of our servants offend in any respect against any man, or transgress any of the articles of the peace or of this security, and the offence is made known to four of the said twenty-five barons, they shall come to us - or in our absence from the kingdom to the chief justice - to declare it and claim immediate redress. If we, or in our absence abroad the chief justice, make no redress within forty days, reckoning from the day on which the offence was declared to us or to him, the four barons shall refer the matter to the rest of the twenty-five barons, who may distrain upon and assail us in every way possible, with the support of the whole

community of the land, by seizing our castles, lands, possessions, or anything else saving only our own person and those of the queen and our children, until they have secured such redress as they have determined upon. Having secured the redress, they may then resume their normal obedience to us. Any man who so desires may take an oath to obey the commands of the twenty-five barons for the achievement of these ends, and to join with them in assailing us to the utmost of his power. We give public and free permission to take this oath to any man who so desires, and at no time will we prohibit any man from taking it. Indeed, we will compel any of our subjects who are unwilling to take it to swear it at our command. If one of the twenty-five barons dies or leaves the country, or is prevented in any other way from discharging his duties, the rest of them shall choose another baron in his place, at their discretion, who shall be duly sworn in as they were. In the event of disagreement among the twenty-five barons on any matter referred to them for decision, the verdict of the majority present shall have the same validity as a unanimous verdict of the whole twenty-five, whether these were all present or some of those summoned were unwilling or unable to appear. The twenty-five barons shall swear to obey all the above articles faithfully, and shall cause them to be obeyed by others to the best of their power. We will not seek to procure from anyone, either by our own efforts or those of a third party, anything by which any part of these concessions or liberties might be revoked or diminished. Should such a thing be procured, it shall be null and void and we will at no time make use of it, either ourselves or through a third party. *

62. We have remitted and pardoned fully to all men any ill-will, hurt, or grudges that have arisen between us and our subjects, whether clergy or laymen, since the beginning of the dispute. We have in addition remitted fully, and for our own part have also pardoned, to all clergy and laymen any offences committed as a result of the said dispute between Easter in the sixteenth year of our reign (i.e. 1215) and the restoration of peace. In addition we have caused letters patent to be made for the barons, bearing witness to this security and to the concessions set out above, over the seals of Stephen archbishop of Canterbury, Henry archbishop of Dublin, the other bishops named above, and Master Pandulf. *

63. IT IS ACCORDINGLY OUR WISH AND COMMAND that the English Church shall be free, and that men in our kingdom shall have and keep all these liberties, rights, and concessions, well and peaceably in their fullness and entirety for them and their heirs, of us and our heirs, in all things and all places for ever. Both we and the barons have sworn that all this shall be observed in good faith and without deceit. Witness the abovementioned people and many

others. Given by our hand in the meadow that is called Runnymede, between Windsor and Staines, on the fifteenth day of June in the seventeenth year of our reign (i.e. 1215: the new regnal year began on 28 May).

Clauses marked (*) were omitted in all later reissues of the charter. In the charter itself the clauses are not numbered and the text reads continuously. The translation sets out to convey the sense rather than the precise wording of the original Latin. Supplied courtesy of the British Library Board.

St. Nicholas' Chapel, Coggeshall, formerly the gatehouse chapel to the original Cistercian Abbey.

THE FIRST FOREST CHARTER OF
KING HENRY THE THIRD

Granted November 6th, A.D. 1217,
IN THE SECOND YEAR OF HIS REIGN.
TRANSLATED FROM THE ORIGINAL, PRESERVED
IN THE ARCHIVES OF DURHAM CATHEDRAL.

HENRY, by the grace of God, king of England, lord of Ireland, duke of Normandy, Acquitaine, and count of Anjou, to the archbishops, bishops, abbots, priors, earls, barons, justiciaries, foresters, sheriffs, governors, officers, and all his bailiffs and faithful subjects, Greeting.

Know ye that we, for the honour for God and for the salvation of our own soul and the souls of our ancestors and successors, for the exaltation of Holy Church and the reform of our realm, have granted and by this present charter have confirmed for us and our heirs for ever, by the counsel of our venerable father, the lord Gualo, T.T. cardinal priest of St. Martin and legate of the apostolic see, of the lord Walter archbishop of York, William bishop of London and the other bishops of England and of William Marshal earl of Pembroke, guardian of us and of our kingdom, and of others our faithful earls and barons of England, these underwritten liberties to be held in our kingdom of England for ever.

1. Imprimis, all the forests made by our grandfather king Henry, shall be viewed by good and lawful men, and if he made any other than his own proper woods into forests to the damage of him whose wood it was, it shall forthwith be disafforested. And if he made his own proper woods forest, it shall remain forest, saving the common (right) of pasturage, and of other things in the same forest, to those who were formerly accustomed to have them.

2. Men who live outside the forest, from henceforth shall not come before our justiciaries of the forest, upon a common summons, unless they are impleaded there or are sureties for any other (persons) who were attached for something concerning the forest.

3. Also all woods which were afforested by King Richard our uncle, or by King John our father, until our own first Coronation, shall forthwith be disafforested, unless they shall be our demesne woods.

4. Archbishops, bishops, abbots, priors, earls, barons, knights and freeholders who have woods within forests shall have them the same as they held them at the time of the first coronation of our grandfather king Henry, (Henry II was first crowned on Sunday December 19th, 1154) so that they shall be discharged forever of all purprestures, wastes, and assarts made in their

84

woods after that time until the beginning of the second year of our coronation. And those who in future shall without our licence make wastes, purprestures or assarts within them, shall answer for such wastes, (purprestures) or assarts. (Waste - cleared but uncultivated worthless land; Purpresture - trespass and erection of dwellings; Assart - land cleared for cultivation).

5. Our regarders shall go through the forests to make a view as it was used to be made at the time of the first coronation of our grandfather, king Henry, and not otherwise.

6. The inquisition or view for lawing of dogs living within the forest, for the future shall be when the view ought to be made, namely, the third year in three years; and then it shall be done by the view and testimony of lawful men, and not otherwise. And he whose dogs shall be found then unlawed, shall give three shillings for mercy, and for the future no one's ox shall be taken for lawing. Such lawing also shall be done by the assize commonly used; which is, that three claws shall be cut off outside the ball of the fore-foot. Nor shall dogs be lawed from henceforth, excepting in places where it hath been customary to expeditate them from the time of the first coronation of king Henry our grandfather. (Lawing or 'expedition' of an animal, especially a dog, was to cut off its claws in order to inhibit deer chasing).

7. No forester nor beadle shall for the future make any scotale, nor collect sheaves of corn or oats, or any grain, or lambs, or swine, nor shall make any gathering but by the view and oath of twelve regarders; and when they shall make their view: as many foresters shall be appointed to keep the forests, as they shall think reasonably sufficient for the purpose. (Scotale - the keeping of an ale-house within a forest by an officer of the forest, who might abuse his position to get trade).

8. No swainmote for the future shall be held in our kingdom, excepting thrice a year; namely, in the beginning of fifteen days before the feast of Saint Michael when the agistators meet for the agisting of our (royal) demesne woods; and about the feast of Saint Martin, when our agistators ought to receive our pannage-dues: and in those two swainmotes the foresters, verderers, and agistators shall meet, and no others by distraint; and the third swainmote shall be held in the beginning of the fifteen days before the Feast of Saint John the Baptist concerning the fawning of our does; and at that swainmote the tenants shall meet the foresters and verderers, and no others shall be distrained to be there. Moreover every forty days through the whole year, the foresters and verderers shall meet for seeing to attachments of the forests, as well of vert as of venison, by the presentment of the foresters themselves and before those who are attached. And the aforesaid swainmotes shall not be holden, except in those

counties where they were accustomed to be held. (Swainmote - a court held before the verderers as judges, by the steward of the court, with swains, freeholders within the forest, making up the jury; Vert - green forest vegetation forming cover or providing food for deer).

9. Every free man shall agist his own wood in the forest as he wishes and have his pannage. We grant also that every free-man may drive his swine through our demesne wood freely and without impediment to agist them in his own woods or anywhere else as he wishes. And if the swine of any free-man shall remain one night in our forest, he shall not on that account lose anything of his for it. (Agist - to pasture livestock for a fee; Pannage - the right to allow pigs to forage in woodland. A fee might be charged for this).

10. No man henceforth shall lose life or limb for taking our venison, but if he shall be seized and convicted of taking venison he shall be fined heavily if he has the means to pay; but if he has not the means, he shall lie in our prison for a year and a day; and if after a year and a day he can find sureties, he shall leave prison; but if not, he shall abjure the kingdom of England.

11. Whatever archbishop, bishop, earl or baron shall be passing through our forest, it shall be lawful for them to take one or two deer under the view of the forester, if he shall be present; but if not, he shall cause a horn to be blown, lest it should seem like theft.

12. Every free-man for the future, may, without being prosecuted, erect a mill in his own wood or upon his own land which he has in the forest; or make a warren, or pond, or marl-pit, or ditch, or turn it into arable land, so that it be not to the detriment of any of the neighbours.

13. Every free-man shall have the eyries of hawks, sparrowhawks, falcons, eagles and herons in his own woods, and he shall likewise have the honey found in his woods.

14. No forester from henceforth, who is not a forester in fee-farm, giving to us rent for his bailiwick, shall take any cheminage, within his bailiwick; but a forester in fee, paying to us rent for his bailiwick, shall take cheminage; that is to say, for every cart two-pence for the one half year, and two-pence for the other half year; and for a horse that carries burdens, one half-penny for the one half year, and one half-penny for the other half year: and not that excepting of those who come out of their bailiwick by licence of their bailiff as dealers, to buy underwood, timber, bark, or charcoal; to carry it to sell in other places where they will: and of no other carts nor burdens shall any cheminage be taken; and cheminage shall not be taken excepting in those places where anciently it used to be and ought to be taken. Also those who carry wood, bark, or coal, upon their backs to sell, although they get their livelihood by it, shall not for the future pay

cheminage. Also cheminage shall not be taken by our foresters, for any besides our demesne woods. (Cheminage - A toll levied on transport in the forest)

15. All persons outlawed for forest offences from the time of king Henry our grandfather up to our first coronation, shall be released from their outlawry without legal proceedings; and they shall find sureties that for the future they will not trespass unto us in our forests.

16. No castellan or other person shall hold forest pleas whether concerning vert or venison but every forester-in-fee shall attach forest pleas as well concerning both vert and venison and shall present them to the verderers of the provinces; and when they have been enrolled and put under the seals of the verderers they shall be presented to our chief forester, when he comes into those parts to hold forest pleas and before him they shall be determined. And these liberties concerning the forests we have granted to all men, saving to the archbishops, bishops, abbots, priors, earls, barons, knights, and others, ecclesiastical as well as secular; Templars and Hospitallers, their liberties and free customs, in forests and outside, in warrens and other places, which they had previously. All these aforesaid customs and liberties which we have granted to be observed in our kingdom for as much as it belongs to us; all our whole kingdom shall observe, clergy as well as laity, for as much as belongs to them. Because we have at present no seal, we have caused the present charter to be sealed with the seals of our venerable father the lord Gualo T.T. cardinal-priest of St. Martin, legate of the apostolic see, and of William Marshal earl of Pembroke, guardian of us and of our kingdom. Witness the before-named and many others. Given by the hands of the aforesaid lord, the legate, and of William Marshal at St. Paul's, London, on the sixth day of November in the second year of our reign.

Copy of the Charter of the Forest supplied courtesy of the British Library Board, and based on the translation in Richard Thomson, An Historical Essay on the Magna Charta of King John, John Major, London, 1829.

Selected Bibliography

Anderson, Verily, *The De Veres of Castle Heddingham*, Terence Dalton, 1993.

Beaumont, G. F., *A History of Coggeshall in Essex*, Marshall Brothers and Edwin Potter, 1890.

Cuddeford, Michael J., Pleshey, *The Origins and History of the Village*, Mount Publications, 1998.

Danziger Danny & Gillingham John, *1215 The Year of the Magna Carta*, Hodder & Stoughton, 2003.

Cooper, Janet, (Editor) *The Victoria History of the County of Essex, Volume IX, The Borough of Colchester*, Oxford University Press, 1994.

Embleton, Paul, *Around Stansted Mountfitchet*, Tempus, 1998.

Greatorex, Jane, *Coggeshall Abbey and Abbey Mill*, Jane Greatorex, 1999.

Greatorex, Jane, *The Benedictine Priory of Castle Hedingham Essex.* Jane Greatorex 2008.

Hallman, Robert, *South Benfleet a History*, Phillimore, 2005.

Hindley, Geoffrey, *The Magna Carta, The Story of the Origins of Liberty*, Constable and Robinson, 2008.

Holt, J.C., *Magna Carta and Medieval Government*, Hambledon Press, 1985.

Ledain, Bélisaire, *Savary de Mauléon et le Poitou à son époque,(Ed. 1892)* Hachette Livre, 2015.

McGlynn, Sean, *Blood, Cries Afar, The Forgotten Invasion of England 1216*, Spellmount, 2013.

Mortimer, Richard, *Angevin England 1154 - 1258*, Blackwell, 1996.

Poole, A. L., *From Domesday to Magna Carta 1087-1216, Second Edition*, Oxford, 1955.

Rackham, Oliver, *The Illustrated History of the Countryside*, Seven Dials, 2000.

Rackham, Oliver, *The Last Forest, The Story of Hatfield Forest*, J.M. Dent & Sons Ltd, 1989.

Rackham, Oliver, *The Woods of South-East Essex*, Rochford District Council, 1986.

Rahtz, Philip, A., *Pleshey Castle, First Interim Report 1960*, Essex Archaeological Society, 1960.

Radulphi de Coggeshall, (Editor Joseph Stevenson), *Chronicon Anglicanum*, Kraus Reprint Ltd, 1965.

Ramsay, Sir James, H. M.A *The Angevin Empire*. Swan Sonnenschein and Co. 1907.

Reaney, P. H., *Essex*, Alfred A. Knoph, 1928.

Round, J. L., *Geoffrey de Mandeville*, Longmans Green and Co, 1892.

Round, J. L (attributed to) *The History and Antiquities of Colchester Castle*, Benham & Co, 1882.

Sinclair, Peter, *Medieval Walkern and Magna Carta*, Walkern History Society, 2013.

Wilson, Derek, *The Plantagenets*, Querus, 2011.

Internet sources

http://magnacarta.cmp.uea.ac.uk/

http://magnacarta800th.com

http://www.bl.uk/magna-cartaBritish Library

The Remains of Pleshey Castle. The Seat of Geoffrey de Mandeville

Authors

ANDREW SUMMERS

Born in East London within the sound of Bow Bells (on a quiet day!), Andrew has lived in Hadleigh for the last 25 years and been married to Glenis for 48 years. Andrew has bought books, sold books, and created an export market selling English language books in Europe. He has also printed books. With a change of tack he has moved on to write and publish books too!

JOHN DEBENHAM

Born in Romford John has always lived in Essex. On retirement from engineering he took a BA History degree at the University of East London, followed by an MA in Intellectual History at Queen Mary, London University where he studied 'Civilisation and Barbarism'. He has an innate curiosity over what makes us what we are, which is satisfied by research, in particular the history of Essex, and writing about it. John is a member of Southend Poetry Society. He writes poetry and short stories with longer works in 'perpetual progress'.

Essex Hundred Publications

Essex Hundred Publications publishes, in the main, a range of Essex centred local history books. A selection can be seen overleaf. By Essex we mean not just the county of Essex as it is today but also the areas of Essex that have been absorbed into London since 1965. The company also distributes a range of local history books from other publishers and has a large portfolio of Essex images.

Essex Hundred authors are also happy to give talks on the subjects published. For further details consult www.essex100.com or e-mail ask@essex100.com

For a list of our titles currently in print please see following two pages.

Essex Hundred Publications

The Essex Hundred
The history of the county of Essex described in 100 poems and supported with historical notes and illustrations.
A unique book written by Essex poets covering 2000 years of county history.
ISBN: 9780955229503 £7.99

Essex Hundred Histories
From the Roman sacking of Colchester to Ford's modern day wind turbines each chapter reflects the diversity of the county as well as showing the role Essex has played in the nation's development.
ISBN: 9780955229510 £8.99
(New edition coming soon)

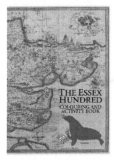

The Essex Hundred Children's Colouring and Activity Book
The Colouring and Activity Book is another title from the Essex Hundred family aimed at children and part written by children. The book includes not only Essex information but pictures to colour in, word searches, puzzles and questions.
ISBN: 9780955229534 £4.99

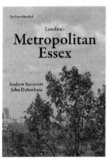

London's Metropolitan Essex
Events and Personalities, from Essex in London, which shaped the nation's history.
ISBN 9780955229558 £12.99

Essex Hundred Publications

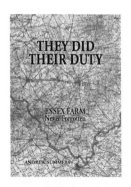

They Did Their Duty, Essex Farm, Never Forgotten by Andrew Summers
A book that tells the story of Essex Farm a First World War cemetery in Belgium that will forever bear the county name and its connections to the Essex Regiment.
ISBN 9780955229596 RRP £9.99

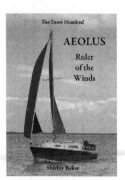

AEOLUS, Ruler of the Winds by Shirley Baker
A whimsical story of sailing adventures around the Essex and Suffolk coast.
ISBN: 9780955229589 £7.99

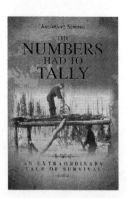

The Numbers Had to Tally by Kazimierz Szmauz
A World War II Extraordinary Tale of Survival
ISBN: 9780955229572 RRP £8.99
(digital edition available)

Essex Hundred Publications. Books written, designed and printed in Essex. Available from bookshops, book wholesalers, direct from the publisher or online. **www.essex100.com**